DRUG ABUSE AND WHAT WE
CAN DO ABOUT IT

DRUG ABUSE AND WHAT WE CAN DO ABOUT IT

Second Printing

Edited by

JAMES C. BENNETT, ED.D.

California State College, Fullerton
Fullerton, California
and
Associate, Southern California Center of Human Behavior
Tustin, California

and

GEORGE D. DEMOS, Ph.D.

California State College, Long Beach
Long Beach, California
and
Director of Drug Abuse Associates
Long Beach, California

CHARLES C THOMAS • PUBLISHER
Springfield • *Illinois* • *U.S.A.*

Published and Distributed Throughout the World by

CHARLES C THOMAS • PUBLISHER

Bannerstone House

301-327 East Lawrence Avenue, Springfield, Illinois, U.S.A.

Natchez Plantation House

735 North Atlantic Boulevard, Fort Lauderdale, Florida, U.S.A.

© *1970, by* CHARLES C THOMAS • PUBLISHER

ISBN 0-398-00132-4

Library of Congress Catalog Card Number: 71-113785

First Printing, 1970
Second Printing, 1972

*With THOMAS BOOKS careful attention is given to all details of
manufacturing and design. It is the Publisher's desire to present books that are
satisfactory as to their physical qualities and artistic possibilities and
appropriate for their particular use. THOMAS BOOKS will be true to those
laws of quality that assure a good name and good will.*

Printed in the United States of America
R-1

FOREWORD

IT IS WELL understood that drug abuse is a major problem affecting our nation. While factual knowledge is becoming more available, practical solutions to alleviate the drug abuse problem are still at the "uncertain" stage. This publication includes factual information and knowledge on an extremely broad basis as discussed by professional persons involved with the problem. Of major importance, practical solutions to alleviate the drug abuse problem are offered and youth are also given the opportunity to express their opinions.

Another significant contribution of this publication is the inclusion of the efforts made by the larger community, in this case Riverside County, California, to come together in order to better understand and to combat the drug abuse problem.

As Superintendent of Schools in Riverside County, it has been my belief that our office is in a strategic position to assist with organizing a coordinated effort to combat the drug abuse problem, and thus we have provided leadership in this area. Also members of our staff have been increasingly concerned about the drug problem among the children and youth of Riverside County. We have worked closely with the school administrators, law enforcement agencies, and many other social agencies in our effort to support the work being done by the leaders of the individual school districts and communities.

Specifically, the Symposium on Drug Abuse Among Youth in Riverside County, which is contained in this publication, was sponsored by our office and was held at the University of California, Riverside Campus, during the early part of 1968. A follow-up workshop entitled "Dangerous Drugs—A Practical Workshop" was held at the Riverside City College in October, 1968, under the sponsorship of Riverside City College in association with the Riverside County Health Department, the California Association for Health, Physical Education and Recreation, and our office.

Another dimension was added to the efforts of the symposium and workshop on drugs when an Ad Hoc Drug Education Committee was formed.

The Ad Hoc Drug Education Committee was charged with the responsibility to serve as a coordinating body of drug information for Riverside County school districts. The Committee has become the communications hub for interchange of drug programs and materials both from within and outside of Riverside County. A wide range of materials dealing with school district policies on drugs, rehabilitation programs, and K-12 curriculum information are available for distribution to the schools in the county.

This commitee is under the leadership of the Counseling—Intergroup Relations—School-Community Services cluster in this office directed by Dr. Lulamae Clemons and is composed of school district personnel selected by the various district superintendents.

We are also pleased to have the parent support as we move toward the solution of the drug problem. It will take the combined help of the school, home, and church, as well as many other social agencies in our broad scale attack on this problem. We need to do much more than we are doing and this publication delineates the direction we should be taking.

Teachers, counselors, administrators, parents and youth are eager to have this kind of material.

Credit is to go to Dr. James Bennett, formerly Assistant Superintendent in Charge of Pupil Personnel Services in our office, and to Dr. George Demos for the excellent work they have done in this publication. Dr. Bennett also originated and formulated the plan for the Symposium and served as the Symposium Chairman.

LEONARD GRINDSTAFF, Ed.D.
Superintendent of Schools
Riverside County, California

CONTENTS

vii

SECTION THREE

CONCLUSION

DRUG ABUSE AND WHAT WE CAN DO ABOUT IT

SECTION ONE

PROCEEDINGS OF A SYMPOSIUM ON DRUG ABUSE AMONG YOUTH IN RIVERSIDE COUNTY, CALIFORNIA

PARTICIPANTS

James C. Bennett, Ed.D.
formerly Assistant Superintendent
Division of Pupil Personnel
Services
Office of Riverside County
Superintendent of Schools
Riverside, California

Charles H. Slaughter, Ph.D.
Associate Professor
Department of Education
California State College
San Bernardino, California

Ben Clark
Riverside County Sheriff
Riverside,California

Eldon Hite
Supervising Parole Agent
California Youth Authority

Clyde Jeffrey
Chief Deputy Probation Officer
Riverside County Probation
  Department
Riverside, California

Patrick Malloy
Public Defender
Riverside County
Riverside, California

Byron C. Morton
District Attorney
Riverside County
Riverside, California

John L. Roberts
Attorney-at-Law
Riverside County Board of
  Education Member
Riverside, California

George D. Demos, Ph.D.
Formerly Dean of Students
California State College
Long Beach, California

Duke Fisher, M.D.
Resident Psychiatrist
UCLA Neuropsychiatric Institute
Los Angeles, California

Morris M. Rubin
Associate Superintendent
Medical Services
California Rehabilitation Center

Fred Veitch, M.D.
Director, Student Health Services
University of California
Riverside, California

Trester S. Harris, M.D.
Staff Physician and Surgeon
California Rehabilitation Center

John C. Kramer, M.D.
Chief of Research
California Rehabilitation Center

John F. McMullin, M.D.
Chief, Department of Psychiatry
Riverside County General Hospital
Riverside, California

5

Clyde A. Pitchford, M.D.
President
Riverside County Medical
   Association
Riverside, California

Thais S. Yeremian, Ed.D.
Coordinator, Counseling and
   Guidance
Office of Riverside County
Superintendent of Schools
Riverside, California

Father Patrick O'Connor
Watkins House
University of California
Riverside, California

Roger Harlow
Child Welfare and Attendance
   Officer
Desert Sands Unified School
   District

Warren T. Randall
Technical Staff
Minuteman Program Office
TRW Systems
San Bernardino, California

Jan Horn
School Psychologist
Riverside Unified School District
Riverside, California

Armon F. Sharp
Supervisory Deputy Probation
   Officer
Riverside County Probation
   Department
Riverside, California

George G. Thomas, Jr.
Supervisory Deputy Probation
   Officer
Riverside County Probation
   Department
Riverside, California

Muriel M. Weiner
Governing Board Member
Desert Sands Unified School
   District

STUDENT PANEL

Eileen Stuve
Alford Unified School District

Jerry Maio
Alvord Unified School Dstrict

Christy Hayes
Beaumont Unified School District

William Terry
Beaumont Unified School District

Eric Asher
Desert Sands Unified School
District

Arthur Torres
Desert Sands Unified School
District

Cammy Larson
Palm Springs Unified School
District

Scott Anderson
Palm Springs Unified School
District

INTRODUCTION

THE PURPOSE OF THIS symposium is to focus our attention on drug abuse among youth in Riverside County, California. In ever-increasing numbers junior and senior high-school youth are using drugs which can be dangerous to physical, emotional and mental health. Effective deterrents to drug use have not been apparent. Students know that by using drugs they may lose opportunities both for a better education and for obtaining employment. Students know that psychological and physical dependence may result from the use of drugs. Students know that felony charges, jail sentences, fines, and criminal records may result from the use of drugs. Even with these understandings, the use of drugs by our youth has continued to grow in both numbers and in the seriousness of the situation by youth and society. The increase in the use of marijuana alone has been startling. We have been told that while marijuana may not cause a physical dependence, it can cause a psychological dependence which can serve as a stepping stone to more serious drug experimentation and possible addiction. With regard to LSD (d-lysergic acid) and "Speed" (amphetamines) we are told that they may cause permanent damage. Whatever the cause or causes, and many are suggested, the continued misuse of drugs by youth is causing increasingly serious problems within our communities.

We in education have a primary involvement. It is our goal to educate youth for individual fulfillment and responsible citizenship. We cannot remain anxiously on the sidelines and see boys and girls jeopardize their present and future lives. What can we do? We can bring together valid information from the various authoritative sources available to create a pool of knowledge for our use. By joining forces, the various agencies, professions, and individuals who are responsible for and responsive to our community can work more effectively in dealing with problems of drug abuse in our country.

7

It is with this in mind that the Office of Riverside County Superintendent of Schools arranged this symposium as a beginning step for dealing with the drug problem. This symposium consists of four parts: Legal Aspects, Medical Aspects, Community Aspects, and the Youth Reaction Panel.

JAMES C. BENNETT, ED.D.

PART I
LEGAL ASPECTS OF DRUG ABUSE

SꜱHERIFF CLARK: There is a tremendous need for people who have a direct connection with the individuals who are most likely to use drugs to join with educators in an attack on this problem. Many times, questions are asked of parents, or in a classroom; it is the lack of ability to answer these questions at the time that really contributes to some of the problems that we have seen.

As far as statistics are concerned, in the past few years we have seen in the County of Riverside about a 600 percent increase in juvenile narcotics arrests. Narcotic arrests have been increasing year after year. Normally the burglary arrests have always led as far as the type of a felony arrest in the state. I mentioned that you will see more and more arrests made locally for a number of reasons. The main one, of course, is that law enforcement is actually doing its job. This crime is one of concealment. You don't have a true victim. If you, for example, are a victim of a burglary, you call a law-enforcement agency and you want something done. In the narcotics violations, the only way that the law-enforcement agency can find the narcotic in the area is to put individuals into the field and try to develop this type of information.

There is a misunderstanding in various groups, school teachers or parents, as to how the law-enforcement agencies handle a reported violation. People assume that as soon as they call a police agency there is going to be a police car in front of the school or the home and an arrest is going to be made, and then everybody is unhappy. But from a realistic standpoint. what we have tried to do, for a number of years, is to encourage the schools and parents to let us know when they see something that is taking place among the youngsters in the home or school as it pertains to this problem. For example, a school teacher in teaching a group of individuals can certainly spot changes in a particular student. Even though the teachers may not have anything to put their finger on, they may suspect narcotics, but the school does not have the time or personnel to check. We, the police, welcome this type of a phone call. We are not going to arrest somebody immediately. We are going to start an investigation. We are interested in the source of the material. As soon as we develop concrete information through an investigative lead or observation, immediate action is going to be taken.

One other problem has to do with the penalty for various narcotic offenses. Normally the punishment ranges between a felony and a misdemeanor. Various violations of marijuana and narcotics laws are felonies, and those dealing with pills and LSD are misdemeanors. There are sections that provide for discretion by the court. The court can set the violations as a felony or a misdemeanor. In the last couple of years, we have seen efforts to legalize the use of marijuana. Also, we have seen a move to reduce the penalty for the possession of marijuana. In my opinion, there should either be a tight control and stringent enforcement, or we should prove that there is no problem with these drugs and then remove the law from the books. One last thing that has to do with a comment I made earlier. It is important to know that law-enforcement agencies are involved in providing order, and the order that they provide is based on the laws that are enacted, and laws are enacted to solve problems in society. It is from this standpoint that we normally operate.

A booklet that was published by the California Delinquency Prevention Commission says "How can we turn the tide?" It says that there is no simple solution to this complex problem, and addiction is unlike preventive medicine which can identify specific symptoms of a disease and prescribe specific preventive measures. Prevention of drug abuse requires an enlightened public understanding of the problem, *good law enforcement,* and adequate treatment resources. Through enforcement of existing laws we must continue the vigorous fight to apprehend those who prey upon others in spreading drug dependence and addiction. We must become more skilled in identifying users and focus on treating the personality defects of the individuals.

We must continue to develop strong preventive programs designed to eliminate factors within a community which contribute to the problem.

DISCUSSION

MR. ROBERTS: Since this is a discussion on the legal aspects, I thought I might mention to you some of the approaches here that perhaps not all of you are acquainted with. As Sheriff Clark has indicated, there are statutes on the books that make different crimes of the conduct of the individual varying from misdemeanors to felonies and carrying all types of sentences. But most paramount in the minds of all those who are connected with the enforcement of these laws is, namely; What is the need of the individual that has been arrested? What is necessary to return this individual to a status of a qualified citizen? For that reason the whole system has been set up whereby when a citizen is arrested, attention immediately focuses on what can we do to rehabilitate the individual. Shall it be simply assessing a fine; shall it be placing him on probation; shall it be commitment to the county jail as a condition of probation and then placement on probation under the supervision of the probation department for two or three years to see whether or not they continue to make further continued violations or whether they rehabilitate themselves, or is it necessary to go farther and make straight commitment to either the county jail, to the youth authority, or to state prison? In doing this, it is the interest of everyone, prosecutor as well as the defense counsel and the court and the probation office.

Their paramount interest is to rehabilitate the individual so that he is not going to be a danger to society or a danger to himself. In some of the lower courts, the muncipal courts as well as the Superior Court, they want as much information about the individual as possible. Having gained a conviction or taken a plea to the charge, the matter is referred then to the county probation department. They then make an investigation and report back to the court where they get all kinds of information. They find out whether this individual has a prior record, whether or not he comes from a broken home, and whether he is beneficially employed. They supply to the court and, of course, the defense counsel is privileged then to add any additional facts that might help guide the court in this respect. So, the point I wish to make is, we have many statutes of different kinds involving the crimes which we are considering primarily here today. But the whole purpose and intent of the judicial system is to rehabilitate the individual and, when he does return to society, to trust that he returns a better citizen than he was at the time he was arrested.

DR. DEMOS: Do you feel that the severity of the punishment is going to have an effect upon the increase or decrease of the narcotic problem?

SHERIFF CLARK: I think that this is something that is highly argumentative. One reason is that in my opinion, we don't really have any true statistics that show either that severe punishment is a deterrent or that the lack of severe punishment is a deterrent. What I am saying is probably best illustrated in the area of capital punishment.

DR. FISHER: I would like to comment on the use of the word narcotic. I think one of the problems is that there is a difference in terms of a legal definition and in terms of a medical definition. Narcotics are opium derivatives like heroin. Marijuana is classified as a narcotic. However, it is actually a hallucinogenic drug. Its classification is the same as LSD, DMT, and STP, except it's much less potent. There is a difference of opinion among law-enforcement officials as to the effectiveness of the severe penalty for marijuana. The chief of the Los Angeles Police Department recently made the statement that he felt that the marijuana laws should be reexamined in the face of possible new research and mentioned the advantage of leaving the choice to the judge in terms of a felony or a misdemeanor.

DR. DEMOS: We're concerned about the credibility gap that exists between the older generation and the younger generation. Many of the young people on our college campuses in particular are very concerned about this apparent inequity in the penalties for certain drugs. We know pharmacologically that marjuana is a relatively benign drug in terms of the scale of its toxicity. At the same time, it is not a narcotic as Dr. Fisher has indicated. We are having enough problems with alcohol, let alone legalizing marijuana; but at the same time, the tremendous impact that a felony arrest can have on a young person, his future career, his inability to enter certain fields should be considered. The onus that a felony arrest has on an individual who may be experimenting with the drug—who may not be a chronic user of marijuana is an example. These are the kinds of questions that young people are asking us. They are looking critically and hostilely toward the law enforcement, the legal profession, and toward society generally for not doing something about the apparent inequities in terms of the penalties. I would go along with Dr. Fisher as indicated that a strong reexamination needs to be made. Many authorities in the field have indicated that this felony penalty is definitely out of line, and I know there are others who indicate otherwise. While from the medical point of view, the use of drugs is something not to be condoned; however, I don't think this comes to grips with the question of the severity of the penalty. We are not asking for it to be legalized. We are asking, however, for it to be more in line with the realistic scene as it is today.

MR. HITE: I would just comment that a great part of this problem is being handled on the local level because the life of a young person is being committed to the youth authority out of Riverside County in addition to the drug use and the background of other delinquency or other criminal activities. We are not having people committed to our agency for possessing one marijuana cigarette. We are having people commited to us, actually for the most part, for delinquent or criminal acts, but who have been involved in narcotics use.

MR. MALLOY: I would like to express agreement with the two gentlemen who disagreed with Sheriff Clark as to the aspect of punishment. We are getting a different type of so-called criminal in connection with violations in the area of use and possession of marijuana in that the defendant is very apt to be, and increasingly more so, not the person who is tainted with the usual attributes of criminality. But this person—young man or young woman—is not a criminal in the sense that we're accustomed. Those of us who are in law enforcement look over the prisoner's box and see, as the cartoons indicate, the sloping forehead and other things that indicate this person is a criminal. You see nice kids, nice-looking, decent college kids. It is the feeling of a good many of us that a severe sentence can destroy a young man or a young woman. For if we are not convinced, as a good many of us are not, that one experience of smoking marijuana is sufficient to constitute a person a criminal, therefore, we're very much concerned about the matter and feel that certainly it's no solution to insist on a felony penalty or punishment.

MR. JEFFREY: I think we should state here that the application of the drug laws differs in the criminal and juvenile courts. The juvenile court in particular has some latitude in dispositions open to it. The juvenile court law applies to all under the age of twenty-one. Between the ages of eighteen and twenty-one, the adult court has the discretion of referring a person to the juvenile court or keeping him in the adult court.

In the adult court, a person is amenable to having any or all the penalties defined in the various legal codes imposed upon him. In juvenile court, however, a person would not be subject to these penalty provisions. This court can apply whatever disposition it feels necessary, taking into account the social and behavioral background as well as the offense. Very important is the fact that a disposition of the juvenile court does not in a legal sense constitute a conviction of a felony.

We have a case involving a student here at UCR who is a 3.78 GPA and a geophysics major. After graduation he has been accepted for graduate study at U.C. Berkeley. To help finance his studies, he was planning to make application for employment at the Linear Accelerator at Hayward. The application asks for any felony convictions. Here is a person, I would say, who has an excellent potential for becoming a valuable contributor to our society and yet he could be excluded from employment in a field related to his interests. Fortunately for this young man, he was nineteen years of age at the time he was arrested for the drug offense, for it gave the adult court the chance to certify his matter for handling in the juvenile court. The non-felony aspect of the juvenile court disposition will be helpful. I think we ought to take this kind of situation into account when we talk about dispositions and applications of the laws as they now exist so far as prevention is concerned.

I am of the opinion that if we feel that rigid, strict, energetically enforced drug laws are going to solve the problem of drug abuse among the young, we are mistaken. Increasing the legal penalties likewise is not the solution. Our greatest hope is to attack the problem at a deeper level. We must discover the incongruities in our society which cause people to try to use artificial means to dissociate themselves from them. We have been neglectful in truly working toward correcting these inconsistencies.

Why do so many young people experiment with drugs? I hope these discussions will help to find the real reason. Then we can begin to find the means of curbing the problem of drug involvement. I would start by repeating that we cannot rely on penalties alone to solve the problem. It is a dangerous oversimplification to say that if we only inform the young people of the severity of the drug laws, the penalties and the intention to enforce them vigorously, the problem will go away. It is our experience that this approach can only antagonize most young people all the more and tend to increase the already existing cleavage between them and authority. Among other things they are aware of wide and accepted use of prescription drugs by their parents to artificially reach a variety of physical and emotional states. They are also aware of other incongruities in the value systems of our society. When they become enough concerned they may not only resort to drug use but as we now know, many feel impelled to aggressively push toward bringing about meaningful changes which the larger society has been reluctant or slow to bring about.

MR. MORTON: I feel that many of our students are not aware of the severity of felony punishment and what can be the consequence of a felony conviction. I think that our schools, our service clubs and our present organizations should educate the parents, as well as the students, that if they are convicted of a felony it goes on their record. When they apply for a job they may not get that job because they have been convicted of a felony. To make it more emphatic, the law does provide that any person who is arrested and possesses a marijuana cigarette, whether it be a whole or a half, or a marijuana plant or a marijuana substance, is guilty of a felony. I don't think these young people realize this. It is up to law enforcement to pass the word on and educate these young people, as well as the teachers and the parents. I don't think that we are communicating this information to them strongly enough.

SHERIFF CLARK: You may find some individual law-enforcement officers who do not agree that there should be reevaluation, but I think that one thing that you will find probably is that a policeman is very practical. When you talk about reevaluation, he is interested in what you are talking about, what you mean by this reevaluation. Who is going to reevaluate and to what extent will the reevaluation go? There is information available but many choose not to believe it. Many want to reshuffle the facts and start a new game, regardless of what discipline they are from or which they effect. Law enforcement will view any study and consider its merits and the stand that has been taken. But also from a practical standpoint, we recognize that while all this study is going on, life will continue. What are we going to do? This is what we're going to do—maintain the existing laws. Another point, as far as the police are concerned, we don't feel that you are going to solve a great deal by removing the person's responsibility for their own personal acts.

WOMAN FROM AUDIENCE: Within the last eight months I have been very disappointed. The laws are on the books, the statutes are there. The police do a great deal of work. Many times, hours and hours are spent before they make an arrest. The arrest is made, the evidence is overwhelming, and in more than just a few instances this has been a probation violation, they have committed the act usually while a second or third time on probation and they are let off in too many cases where the law hasn't been implemented in the court room, and it must be terribly frustrating to the peace officers who put in so many hours.

The Grand Jury of Marin County and some other grand juries, and, I think, some legislators advocate that the court have a discretion as to whether or not the possession of marijuana is either a felony or a misdemeanor.

DR. EDWIN GARDNER, RETIRED M.D. AND RIVERSIDE COUNTY BOARD OF EDUCATION MEMBER (FROM AUDIENCE): I am rather shocked to hear any person make a statement that marijuana is a relatively benign drug. It is not. There are many many cases on record of insanity because of the use of marijuana or hashish. We're getting hashish into the United States at the present time. When you talk about drugs that are difficult to control, I would call your attention to the fact that there are many nations which do not allow marijuana to be used at the present time and when you experience a cutdown on the penalty you can make up your mind you're going to get more and more use. Would any person making the statement that youngsters should experiment like to have an experiment that would terrorize them right away?

DR. DEMOS: I don't think anyone said that a youngster should experiment with drugs. The statement made that young people *are* experimenting with drugs and are frequently not chronic users, but perhaps individuals who have heard about what these drugs will do will try it once. Frequently these individuals are apprehended. Now, secondly, the question of marijuana being a benign drug was reported by Dr. David Smith, pharmacologist, formerly with the Berkeley Medical School and presently running the Haight Ashbury Clinic in San Francisco. Perhaps you are talking about hashish which is a much more potent form of this particular drug and usually the kind of marijuana that is prevalent in this country is not as potent as hashish. I don't think anyone, however, is recommending that young people experiment with any of these drugs.

DR. EDWIN GARDNER: There is one thing I would like to call to your attention. If you check the eyes of a person who is using marijuana, in most instances, you will find he has dilated pupils. If any of you people here wearing glasses ever had drops put in your eyes when you were younger, you know the difficulty you had in seeing. Any person, I don't care how old, that uses marijuana and has dilated pupils, can't judge distance. It reaches a point where their system is affected from marijuana whether it may be the benign type you have mentioned or the hashish. You can see that when they go out on the road with an automobile they are just as dangerous as any person under alcohol.

DR. DEMOS: That is correct. Let me say one other thing. I agree with that last statement. I don't disagree with the fact that using alcohol and driving or using marijuana and driving can be dangerous. I do want to emphasize the point that imposing penalties frequently allays our guilt feelings and consciences and somehow we believe we're solving the problem by imposing stiff penalties. It's far from solving the problem, and we have to do the much more difficult task of working toward prevention. And this is where, I think, we have been definitely remiss. We've had a tendency to impose penalties and let the law-enforcement people handle it instead of us trying to do everything we can to educate young people about the possible damage of drug abuse.

MR. LUXTON, RIVERSIDE COUNTY JUVENILE HALL TEACHER (FROM AUDIENCE): We're talking about how strict penalties on students may deter their future development. Could you explain Mr. Jeffrey or Mr. Morton or Mr. Roberts about "expungement." Does this exist? I heard about it quite a bit from the probation people I work with and I'm not really familiar with this and if this does exist would this aid the student?

MR. ROBERTS: There is expungement of records both in adult court and juvenile court. However, the juvenile expungement is one I think we should address ourselves to, primarily because if the court takes an action for expungement in a juvenile court matter it erases it. The young people or the individual involved can answer "No" to a question, "Have you a juvenile record?" But the requirements are that the person has been out of the jurisdiction of juvenile court for five years or upon reaching the age of twenty-one, whichever occurs first. Then he can apply for the expungement. It's not automatic and investigation is made, and then also I neglected to say that if during the period between the time the jurisdiction concludes and the time he is eligible he has not been convicted of a felony or a misdemeanor involving moral turpitude, he qualifies. If there is some conviction like that he does not qualify.

MR. LUXTON (FROM AUDIENCE): May I make a further comment. You say that he can get the expungement on application. Suppose that after expungement the juvenile court record is eradicated. I was talking to an employer yesterday at a local market and we were talking about expungement and I said what if the boy, after obtaining expungement, would place on his application: "I have no previous court record,"—and they found out through one means or another that he had committed a felony. What would they do? How would you get around that?

MR. ROBERTS: This section of the law provides that a copy of the order of expungement would be sent to each agency which had record of the person's juvenile arrest. I emphasize juvenile. Upon receipt of the order, each agency is to expunge the person's juvenile arrest record and, in a sealed envelope, verify to the court that this was done. But I also hasten to say the Federal Bureau of Investigation will not honor this. The C.I.I. (Bureau of Criminal Identification and Investigation) in Sacramento would honor it though. We can, however, if we want to pursue it, ask the agency that submitted the record to the F.B.I. request that it be withdrawn (and to my knowledge the F.B.I. record would be dropped.)

I might point out that even with regard to adults, or boys eighteen to twenty-one that are being treated as adults by the court, in placing them on probation rather than confinement or even where confinement is a condition of probation, if they perform according to the terms of their probation by the expiration of the probation period, they can go back into court and move the court for the privilege of changing their plea from guilty to not guilty and have the matter dropped. There is sta-

tutory provision for this and again it's part of the same prin-
ciple of trying to give the individual an opportunity to rehabilitate himself and as such then he doesn't stand convicted of the
crime of a felony or a misdemeanor as the case may be, but he
can then answer on his record when he is applying for a job that
he has *not* been convicted of a felony.

If the question is worded, "Have I been arrested?" he would
have to say "yes." In the juvenile thing he could still say "No."
There is a little bit of difference there. With some of the other
laws that have been proposed in the last two years about sealing a record, this is an aside. If you think we have trouble with
a credibility gap now, what do you think it would be like when
you start telling people that even though they were arrested
they weren't arrested?

MR. JEFFREY: The purpose of rehabilitation is to change
them back to what they were and you're saying they were already law breakers. Would you like to react to that?

MR. ROBERTS: I think his point is well taken. The thing
that he may have reference to in one part of the question has
to do with some studies that were conducted a few years ago.
And by a few years ago, the last one that I am aware of ended
about 1955, and the conclusion was, and this is an oversimplification, that all criminals may not be addicts but all addicts are
criminals. This, of course, has been indicated, I think, by a
number of comments here this morning, and we see some difference as far as various people who are using narcotics. Los Angeles
City, about a year ago, released some figures that dealt with
the crime of burglary, and I believe, and here I am relying on
my memory, about 80 percent of the burglaries were committed
by people who were using narcotics or who were addicts. I
think you'll find that when many students are arrested for possession, it is their first offense, and many times they have never
been convicted of any other crime. It seems they got in the
wrong association or the wrong crowd or they were out with
somebody and they happened to be arrested with them. These
are the people, I think, that the proponents of the reduction of
the marijuana punishment are looking toward because these

persons are first offenders with no other criminal record. I think the proponents of this adjustment of the penalty are looking toward these first offenders because they don't feel that felony punishment is justified.

MODERATOR: I would like to ask Sheriff Clark and Mr. Morton both, Do you feel that school personnel are cooperating with you as you would have them cooperate at this time?

SHERIFF CLARK: From a personal standpoint at this time I would say yes. Two months ago or, say, twelve months ago, I'd have had much more reservation about giving this unqualified answer.

DR. FISHER: The widespread use of marijuana is making it difficult to brush its use aside as deviant behavior. A U.C.L.A. questionnaire found that almost 50 percent of the undergraduate population at one time had tried marijuana. I have done some informal polls of high schools in the West Los Angeles area. One poll idicated the marijuana use (one or more trials) to be around 70 percent. We could say that only 30 percent have nondeviant behavior, but I think we are saying that there are many students who use marijuana socially or on a one time experiment. Many times it is the curious student who isn't a dropout and who isn't antisocial, but tries marijuana because it is the "in" drug. And I think the question that is being brought up here is that the law is not taking this into consideration.

MODERATOR: I want to make one statement. The probation services advisory committee, and I believe an interim committee, is actually doing some work on the expungement problem. It creates a very real problem as far as employment is concerned and the legislature this year is concerning itself with the problem of expungement.

GENTLEMAN FROM THE AUDIENCE: I'd like to throw in several factors and probably direct these to Dr. Demos. I think we should be cognizant of this fact in particular, that we paint the picture of a clean-cut real fine young American boy in college who is using a marijuana cigarette—the poor boy. You are going to protect this boy. Now who gets arrested? Is it the guy at the party that's arrested? I've interrogated Sheriff Clark's department and the local police department and it is not. The majority of these people getting arrested are individuals who commit crimes on the street as a result of using marijuana. These are the people the law should be set up for, and not these poor little innocent boys that you paint the picture of on the campus.

PART II
MEDICAL ASPECTS OF DRUG ABUSE

D R. RUBIN: Dr. Norman Shumway at Stanford didn't have as hard a job doing his heart replacement operation as we have in trying to cure a heroin drug addict of his addiction! Drug abuse and drug addiction are, as you well know, not medical problems alone. The legal, the sociological, and educational phases of these problems are just as important as the medical or psychiatric. We will attempt to reach a point of reference in viewing the problem by presenting for your consideration and acceptance a definition of drug addiction and of drug abuse. Perhaps both may be a matter of degree of dependence. We will mention most of the drugs involved in addiction and abuse and say a brief word about their properties as we know them today. And lastly, we would like to know about the rapidly increasing medical complications we are now seeing as the result of the indiscriminate and improper use of the hypodermic needle to get the drug under the skin or into the vein.

DRUG ADDICTION

I think drug addiction may be considered to be the compulsive and repetitious use of the drug in which the person has lost the power of self-control with reference to the drug and abuses it to the extent that the person or society is harmed. Its characteristics are principally three: (1) *Tolerance*: The ability of the host to tolerate increasing amounts of the drug and the requirement for affect. (2) *Psychological dependence*: Habituation or compulsion to continue the drug and obtain it by almost any means. (3) *Physiological dependence*: An alteration in the body physiology so that withdrawal symptoms may result when the drug is suddenly discontinued. The California Legislature has acknowledged the condition of drug dependence legally termed, "imminent danger" of addiction which is rather difficult to define medically, but which can be recognized by an examining physician who obtains a careful medical history, does a complete physical examination, and has certain laboratory tests performed. On the basis of imminent danger to addiction, an individual may be ordered to civil commitment at the California Rehabilitation Center. Now, we will speak of the abuse of drugs.

THE ABUSE, OR MISUSE OF DRUGS

This is the act of indiscriminately using therapeutic or nontherapeutic drugs or chemicals without the proper supervision or prescription of a physician or one scientifically acquainted with the drugs. As in the addiction definition, the drug may, and often does interfere with the abuser's health, economic situation, or social adjustment. The drugs misused are (1) *the opiates,* and these are the drugs most frequently connected with addiction—we call these the hard narcotics; (2) *the sedatives and tranquilizers;* (3) *the stimulants,* and (4) *hallucinogens.* I personally put marijuana in a class by itself, because marijuana has no truly therapeutic effect. Drug abusers, like narcotic addicts may develop increasing tolerance for their drugs—emotional dependence and possibly some degree of physical dependence. The principal difference is that the addict suffers an almost overwhelming enslavement. This, in effect, means that though dependence may have been established, the abusers will not go to the extreme ends the addicts will go to obtain their drugs. In other words, they have not yet lost the power of self-control. Bear in mind that we are dealing with two primary factors: (1) the infecting organism, and it is extremely variable; you heard from the discussion this morning about marijauna and hashish; (2) the susceptible host, which also is extremely variable.

Now what are the drugs specifically? First the opiate, and that means a drug derived from the opium poppy. Morphine was the first one synthesized from opium and this came about in 1805 in Germany. Then came codeine, and you are no doubt familiar with it, in the year 1832 in France. And then in 1898, Germany came out with a "nonaddicting" drug almost as good as morphine, called heroin. We also have in this same group, paregoric. These other drugs are not too often involved, but they are addicting drugs. Now there are certain synthetic equivalents of the opiate drugs. Demerol® came out in 1936, and I remember it so well. It was supposed to be a nonaddicting drug, and I prescribed it with that idea. We soon learned that it *was* an addictive drug. And today when a doctor becomes addicted to drugs it is usually Demerol. In this same group is percodan (a very dangerous drug), methadone, pethizocine and oxycodone. Now methadone is being used in some areas to treat narcotic addiction. The last one in the group is cocaine. Cocaine is primarily a stimulant that gives you a sense of euphoria and it causes little physical dependence.

The sedatives are the second group. The sedatives include the barbiturates: phenobarbital, nembutal, seconal, tuinal, pentothal, and all those household drugs almost as common as aspirin. Also included with the sedatives are the tranquilizers. Some people take tranquilizers like some of you eat popcorn. A stress situation comes up and you take two or three Equanil® or Miltown® and then you start to face your problem. Along with the sedatives in the next subgroup are the bromides. These include Bromo-Seltzer, Nervine, Neurosene, and triple bromides, and some of these drugs are found in the go-to-sleep-quick things we see on television. The next group contains the drugs paralderyde and chloralhydrate and I include alcohol in this same area.

The stimulants are the third big group. These are the amphetamines, the pep pills that we know are so very dangerous. These include Benzedrine® and Bendzedrex® which are contained in some of these sniffers to shrink the mucous membranes in your nose (some people take those things out and eat them) dexedrine, methedrine and others. Methedrine we now call "speed"—the San Francisco special. And two weeks ago I learned that Nodoze® has been added to this list. It is not a narcotic, or a hallucinogen, but NoDoze is being misused. Fourth is the *hallucinogens*. Some may sound strange; peyote, mescaline, psilocybin, morning glory seed, and LSD. Dr. Fisher can tell you so much more about those. Then comes DMT, dimethyltryptamine, STP, and lastly solvent-sniffling. What a menu to choose from! Marijuana (you heard a little about this morning) is known as

Cannabis sativa. That's its technical name, and briefly I can say that in 2700 BC it was described in a Chinese pharmacopia. It's the Indian hemp plant. It has intoxicating qualities that we know, but there are no known therapeutic effects.

The smoking of marijuana was introduced into the United States from Mexico about 1910, principally down in New Orleans. I guess it faded out and now it has come back in the way we know it. Marijuana, far from the harmless drug it is considered by many, can cause extreme disorientation and may cause psychosis.

Very quickly I want to enumerate the medical complications which we now encounter because of the need to get the drug in quick, under the skin, and preferably into the vein—the main line. First is *overdose.* An intravenous injection of a drug sends a full load of it directly, within a split second of time, to the heart, the lungs, and the brain. These vital centers may be knocked out almost immediately and it is not infrequent for the police officers to find a dead addict with the needle still in his vein. Death came almost instantaneously. The next complication we see is *hepatitis.* This extremely grave liver disease is usually caused by a virus which requires intense heat under controlled pressure to kill it. The addicts who pass their kits from person to person cannot be bothered about autoclaving, sterilizing, or even rinsing their needles and syringes. Third, *endocarditis,* a serious disease of the heart valves caused usually by staphylococcic organisms as well as others which again are passed from user to user by the hypodermic syringe. *Tetanus* is fortunately a very rare complication because of the widespread practice of immunization with tetanus toxoid, and I imagine everyone in this room has been immunized with tetanus toxoid. It is a dreadful thing to see a patient die of lockjaw—tetanus. *Abcesses, phlebitis* and *blood poisoning* are seen very often in such large hospitals as the Los Angeles County General Hospital where large numbers of addicts are admitted for treatment. Now these conditions are also due directly to the bacteria found in the filthy hypodermic outfit, and I'll conclude by saying this: What a hellishly fearful price to have to pay for the euphoria or bang or charge one receives from the jab!

DR. HARRIS: The California Rehabilitation Center was organized in 1961 for the sole purpose of rehabilitating narcotic addicts. It is not a punitive institution. The people whom we consider, whom the judges consider, and who require punishment of any sort are sent to other institutions. We have at the present time about 310 women and about 1800 men in the institution and they come from various parts of California. Eighty percent of them are from southern California, sixty-five percent to seventy percent are from Los Angeles County alone. They have been guilty not only of some narcotic infringement, but of some other felonious charges. We don't have a group of angels there at all. They're put in in order not only to rehabilitate them from their narcotic use, but to make them better citizens, so that when they are turned loose they will eliminate some of their criminal activities. When we figure that each narcotic addict requires a minimum of five injections of heroin a day, or five fixes as they call it, over a period of years (in one year, that makes 1,825), in ten years it equals 18,250 injections at $5.00 each. That runs around $90,000. For these addicts who are not about to take care of themselves or their family while they are addicted, it means that they must steal, burglarize or in some way acquire merchandise to the extent of about $400,000 in order to pass it off to fences for enough money to carry them all. Now you may think that ten years is a long time for someone to be addicted, but we have had any number of fellows in their sixties who have had thirty years of addiction and used more than five fixes a day. In thirty years that amounts to more than a quarter of a million dollars, and you can see how much burglarizing had to be done in order to acquire that much money.

What we do at the center is to educate some of these individuals. It is surprising how many have not completed their elementary and high-school education. In June of 1967, we granted high-school certificates to forty-seven individuals and elementary school certificates to 166. There again you might be surprised to know that there are some people in their twenties and thirties, who are just now having an opportunity to learn to read and to write. In addition to their education, we have a vocational program. These people have an opportunity to learn upholstering, building maintenance, laundry, dry cleaning, gardening, typing, and domestic work. There are any number of things that they can learn and the majority of them are in a program so that when they are able to be released from our institution they can make a living for themselves and their family.

Another thing that we try to do is to rehabilitate them from a physical standpoint. We repair their hernias; we remove tumors, remove unsightly tattoos, and fix them so that when they do get out they will be more acceptable to possible employers in the State of California. When these people are released, they sign an affidavit that they will abide by thirteen very strict rules as a part of their probation. Only one of these rules has to do with narcotic addiction, so the majority of people who are returned to the institution in less than three years are returned for the infraction of one of these other twelve specifications, particularly alcoholism. So when one of the individuals released returns in a few months, we don't consider it a failure. We consider it an opportunity to give a little further treatment, a little further training and give them a better opportunity to mature. The majority of these people are in there because they are not mature. You would be surprised how immature an individual in his thirities can be.

The secret of the success at California Rehabilitation Center was probably forecast years ago by Robert Burns who said, "O, would some power give us the right to see ourselves as others see us." The secret there is in group therapy similar somewhat to the alcohol anonymous program that has been instituted across the country. These individuals are given an opportunity to change their perspectives. They will take suggestions and corrections from their peers that they wouldn't take from members of the staff. If we tried to point out to them the difficulties that they have and the reasons for their difficulties, including their behavior and the way that they attempt to solve their personal problems, they wouldn't accept it at all. But in the group which consists of about fifty in the women's department and about sixty in the men's, these people really pour it on each other and they point out their faults in no uncertain terms. The groups are held each day. Each resident is required to attend the group each day. The success of it, I think, is exemplified by the fact that over four hundred residents have been rehabilitated to a point where they are completely off the program and are out on their own. Now, of course, cold statistics don't tell the whole story. These are human beings, they are individuals with families and everyone who is in there has probably caused a disruption within the family.

To summarize, what we do at the Rehabilitation Center is to give them educational opportunities that they haven't had before—plus vocational training. Many of them have never made a living in their lives as they haven't had the means of being able to make a living. We may have saved their lives because the mortality rate in narcotic addiction and drug addiction in general is fifteen times that of the nonaddict. We frequently read in the paper where a Hollywood model was found dead on the floor of her apartment through an overdose of drugs. Practically every week someone has an overdose. So if we can rehabilitate them or take them off the drugs, we may have saved their lives.

DISCUSSION

DR. McMULLIN: A comment was made in the earlier panel that the laws that have been passed in regard to the control of narcotics and other drugs have been passed as a result of medical knowledge. I regret that this is not the fact. By and large our laws have been passed at a time of crisis and in a state of hysteria. We then find that perhaps the laws we have passed have been in error, at least in part, and it becomes rather difficult for lawmakers to change the law. In any attempt to change the law and perhaps bring it closer to what the medical facts are, the lawmaker is put in the position of being on the side of sin, and this is certainly very difficult for an assemblyman or a senator who has to come back for election.

Unfortunately, because of a certain set of circumstances which started back in the early part of this century, the control of drugs and drug abuse have been largely in the hands of the police and law enforcement. There has been a voluntary abrogation of the responsibility of the medical profession for most of the last fifty years. This voluntary abrogation of the responsibility has been further enhanced by laws that make it very difficult for physicians to treat patients who are drug users. Because of the laws, the drug users are hesitant to come to doctors for they feel they may be turned in, and in fact there is a law on the books in the State of California which requires a physician treating an addict to turn his name in to the state narcotic authorities. I think it is a matter which bears some discussion. The medical profession has *not* been involved very much in the problems of drug abuse. There have been a small number of pioneers who through the years have maintained an interest in it. The numbers have been so small that they might be counted perhaps on one's hands and toes. I think that in the last five or eight years the number has increased, and there are many people, many physicians, psychologists, etc., throughout the country who are becoming interested. We are beginning to do some work in this field and perhaps will indeed in the future, unlike in the past, influence some of the legislation and some of the general thinking and bring it more closely to what the scientific and medical facts are.

I would like to address myself to the problem as we see it here, to the person who is suddenly overwhelmed by drugs to the point where he requires hospitalization. We in the past five and a half years have been in a position to see these cases as brought to the *County General Hospital,* and I want to address myself particularly to the idea of treatment expectations. Perhaps the drug addict himself is not so unrealistic and maybe he even has a rather negative attitude with regard to treatment. But not so the members of his family. They have a high expectation that there is a specific cure, that it can be given, and they don't want to look facts in the face. The sad truth is that the biggest addiction problem that we as physicians have dealt with over the years, and with relatively poor success, is the addiction to alcohol. And this has been a tremendous problem in this country with five or six million people who are alcoholics and perhaps others haven't quite reached that destination yet. But in any event, I don't think we can even look on marijuana as another harmless drug like alcohol. *Alcohol is by no means a harmless drug.* If you had my job and had to see the ravages of alcohol every day, and I don't mean just the alcoholics, but what it does to people and how it contributes to their overall decomposition, then you would not have the idea that alcohol is a harmless drug.

There are too many factors operating against it to do much of a job in alcoholism other than education. The same is true about drugs. If we are ever going to do anything about addiction to the many types of drugs, not just narcotic drugs, but all types of drugs, we will have to do it in the area of education. This is what we consider the role of primary prevention in psychiatry and in mental health. That before one ever gets exposed to these or ever uses them for the first time, he must have been educated, to what the situation is, what these drugs are, what they do. Here again I think this becomes the role of the educator and those in charge of health education programs.

I do feel that right now perhaps we are concentrating too heavily on one or two drugs. We are dramatizing it by selecting LSD and marijuana above all others, forgetting our "old friend" alcohol and forgetting the barbiturates. Who are the people who abuse barbiturates and amphetamines and stimulants? Very often the middle-aged housewife who runs from doctor to doctor getting a prescription here and a prescription there or maybe even running down to Mexico and getting a bottle of her favorite pills. A person like this you would never put in a category of a lawbreaker and yet some of them have been picked up at the border, lost their cars, and have been faced with federal charges of smuggling. So this is, I think, where we have to place our major efforts, i.e., in the role of primary prevention and education. I think we would do best to include this as a bigger program in the schools that would include sex, hygiene, cigarette smoking, alcohol and drug abuse. I think it is more palatable, more saleable when wrapped up in that package than if it were just emphasized that this is marijuana or this is heroin, because most of the kids say that doesn't apply to me, but they are all interested in the other things because they see them. They see alcohol being abused. They know there are sex problems.

The other thing I think that comes up is the tremendous role that the rehabilitation agencies must play. I think the probation department has a tremendous chore added because the majority of first offenders, the early users of habit forming drugs do get placed on probation. They are placed under the probation department and the load on them must be very heavy. There again I think it is a matter of expansion of an inservice training program to enable those people to do their jobs better and provide them the resources they need because they are the ones who are handling the offenders. We must not get hysterical on this and pass a lot of bad legislation. Some of it is in need of revision right now and I think we are or have reached some agreement or some consensus on that.

DR. DEMOS: We were talking about publications that are good. There is an excellent volume by Smith, Cline and French in conjunction with the FDA called *Drug Abuse,* which I would also encourage you to get.

A couple of points that I would like to make are in terms of the students' reactions to the use of drugs—perhaps you're not familiar with the approach that seems to be prevalent in some areas in Los Angeles County, in particular, and that is the "grab bag party" in which young people, as they walk in the front door of a party, reach in and take two kinds of drugs—they are not sure what it is but they just "pop" these pills. Most people are not aware of this kind of abuse that is gaining considerable prevalence among teenage cultures. Where do they get these drugs? We find that most of them are obtained from their own medicine cabinets. The pharmaceutical companies and the medical profession perhaps need to reexamine the question of prescription drugs. Many people are indiciating that the major thrust of the drug abuse problem is not coming from the pushers, but is coming from parents and medicine cabinets in your own homes. You know we haven't been very good models in this regard. How many drugs have you had during the past twenty-four hours? I suspect that most of you have used three or four, maybe five, if you had caffeine or sleeping pills, a cigarette or a drink last night. You've imbibed in a considerable amount of drug usage. Young people realize that there is a certain kind of magic in those pills. It does something to us. It must be good. Recently the American Pharmaceutical Company was found on our campus distributing a drug called "Verve" and this drug theoretically made students brighter—created a way in which people could learn faster and learn more and wake up and profit more from their education (so said the package) and they were distributing these on our campus, to our dismay, until we found out and asked them to leave. They were distributing these capsules and students were taking handfuls because if one would make him smart perhaps five or six or seven would really do the trick. Actually, they were comparable to NoDoz tablet, a caffeine derivative, which people were taking in great amounts.

It is true that young people are imbued with this concept that there is magic in those pills. It will do something for me. Take it for anything. What happened to the concept of signal anxiety, and I would like to ask this of the physicians here. What is wrong with a little anxiety? What does it do to us? The psychiatrist, in particular, isn't some anxiety a good thing? A certain degree of it at least. Why do we have to be so tranquilized? Isn't it desirable for us to have some anxiety to bring about changes—needed changes in our environment? I think that the approach needs to be emphasized to a greater degree in dealing with the question of drug abuse. Why are young people resorting to drugs in epidemic proportions? All kinds of drugs as were indicated here. It's amazing to me, the ingenuity which young people have in experimenting with all kinds of combinations. Frequently they are the real authorities about these drugs. They know what drugs will do and won't do better than anyone, and if you want to know about drugs frequently you go to the drug users and ask them because there is such little quantity of research being done.

At any rate we need more opportunities for the physicians to advise young people that they don't need drugs of this kind. There are better ways of coping with problems. There are ways in which they can become better people by not dropping out, but by coping with problems directly. There is no substitute for hard work and confrontation and there is no magic in pills. It is not going to solve our problems. Unfortunately young people are reluctant to go to the physician, however—reluctant to go to the clergyman and reluctant to go to the teacher or counselor.

In one large school district in Los Angeles County, the director of guidance has a published statement that states very explicitly—any counselor who comes in contact with an individual who is using drugs is to report it to the local police. Is it any wonder that these young people do not come for help and are reluctant to talk about their concern about drugs and why they are using drugs. I think such edicts by some school districts are part of the reason why restrictive and stringent legislation has in a sense driven the problem underground. The physician, the counselor, the teacher, the responsible adult, the clergyman, all need to be available and open to talk with young people with *impunity*. They can level with you about drugs, about the drugs that they are using or contemplating using, and you can talk with them and confront them when needed. I think that this is the approach we need to intensify greatly.

QUESTIONS AND ANSWERS

QUESTION: I wonder if a panel member could indicate whether there has ever been any research on whether original marijuana addiction leads to hard drugs and if there actually has been a study on this?

DR. DEMOS: To my knowledge there have been some studies that show that many users of other drugs, such as hard-core narcotics and, in some instances, psychedelic drugs, were former users of marijuana. However, as far as a direct causal relationship, that is, that there is something inherent in marijuana that causes one to go on to other drugs, that has never been proven.

I think most people feel that this is a myth. It is true that most chronic multiple drug users have at some time used marijuana, but that doesn't mean that because of the marijuana they want other drugs. Certainly, if one is given drugs like marjuana you are exposed to sources of other drugs. And I think only from that viewpoint can you say you get the drug habit.

PART III
COMMUNITY ASPECTS OF DRUG ABUSE

Dr. Yeremian: What is the role of education in the drug abuse problem? What are our educational objectives in this area? We must define these goals not in theoretical terms, but rather with specific behavioral objectives. Whatever program the educational establishment sets forth, it should be in terms of the learner's behavior. It must be observable and it must be measurable, if we are to ascertain the level of achievement of these objectives. To educate the student about drug abuse is not enough. This lacks the concrete specificity that educational objectives must have. To provide a unit on drug abuse in science, social studies, or physical education is not enough. For what we have heard today are the feelings, the facts and concerns of individuals who are deeply aware of the drug abuse problem.

Let me share some of my concerns as an educator. Most of these concerns are really questions that need answers. If we can determine educational objectives regarding drug abuse, how do we achieve them? By what concepts can we reach our goals? Is drug abuse a problem that should be handled by the schools? Is it appropriate for inclusion in the educational program? If so, how do we include it? Where do we begin the information-giving to the students? This morning we heard several comments that it should be given much earlier than we are doing at the present time. If it is not appropriate for the school program, what societal institutions will help the individual to understand drug misuse? The state mandates the unit on narcotics. This has not effectively resulted in an enlightened citizenry if one looks at the drug abuse statistics. However, again, we cannot measure what might have happened if there had been no such unit.

Should drug abuse be a part of a curriculum? If a part, where? How much information should be given to students? Who should teach these units? What kind of in-service training should there be for the teachers or whoever does the teaching? Is there something missing in the present curriculum? Perhaps

43

it should not be specifically a curriculum problem? Could it be handled better through pupil personnel services in the counseling and guidance area? What if counselors were trained in this area for group guidance?

If, as some of the research indicates, the young people who misuse drugs are alienated, uncommitted, disaffiliated personalities of our time; this is the problem we should attempt to solve. What is our role in education? Should the pupil personnel and psychological services have the functions of helping the students become aware of the seriousness of the decision pertaining to drug abuse and the possible consequences of such a decision? Where does the student best learn that vital decisions should not be made in terms of emotion and social pressures, but rather in the light of knowledge and wisdom?

Where, in or out of education, will the most meaningful dialogue take place on drug abuse? Have social values really changed? Is there really a generation gap? Does it have anything to do with drug abuse? Do we care about the policies or are we only concerned with the results? How do we develop human beings who are resistant to drug abuse? What can education do for the alienated students?

Where education has failed in its attempt to teach students the hazards of drug abuse, or the student has turned off the establishment and chosen the drug abuse path, what is the educator's role? What kind of policy can the school district develop that would be constructive for the offender when he returns to school? Or is he allowed to return to school? Should the policy be punitive? How punitive? Is there a need for special schools and special programs for these students who violated the law? What are we going to do with them? What about the prospective students? What effective school policy covers this area of guilt by association? Are these two policies—one written and one actually practiced? Should the punishment be given out to him in the courtroom? Does it begin and end there? Where does punishment for illegal use of drugs fit into the educational philosophy and how do we specifically handle it in the school districts and in the individual school?

Can we formulate an educational program that will be meaningful to the students today? Can this program be constantly modified to keep up with the current research findings in the medical professions? If we are in a period of time where man has found that dominating his environment is the way to worldly achievement it is essential that we in education know where we are going, what our goals and objectives are and the process for achieving these objectives. We must utilize all of the resources available and include all areas of concern to the individual.

FATHER O'CONNOR: I would like to start with sort of a fable, although it's taken from a modern day film called "Blow Up," by the Italian producer Antonini. Antonini, in the film "Blow Up," catches the spirit of the "mod" society and modern-day London and in one scene in the film, the young photographer—who the film centers around—goes to a teenage discotheque and he watches the musicians play. He stands among the teenagers and suddenly the group on the stage with their electric guitars and drums begin tearing up their instruments to achieve more sound, fury, whatever. And the scene becomes a real mad orgy of pandemonium. There is another scene of this film, where we find the group of young people cruising around the city of London on the back of a truck and they stop at a park, walk through the park to a tennis court and begin to play tennis. They are using an imaginary tennis ball and play very slowly and play in sort of a tranquil mood.

Now I think both scenes, the frenzy of the discotheque and the slow-motion cadence of the imaginary tennis game, capture the spirit, in a way, of modern-day youth. And I think both are validly symbolic of something that is going on in our society. All the way from the wild boisterous rock rhythms and discotheques to the slow tranquil cadence of the drug scene—young people are escaping from and reacting to the society around them. Both are produced by the society they spring from. I don't think we should fall into the age-old trap of roundly and arrogantly condemning the young because of this escape or because of this reaction. Now this is neither to condone nor to down-phrase the frightening spread, if you will, of drugs, and all the other kinds of pills and escapes in our modern society from the adult right down to the young man. It is only an attempt to locate the action and put it in its right perspective. And I think the challenge is *pointed out* from all this, the challenge to you and to me, to responsible adults, educators, teachers and law enforcement people and clergymen. I think the challenge that comes to us is this: *How do we convince them that our world, the world they are escaping from, is any more real than their world?*

It is easy for us to say that their world, the drug-induced world, or maybe the mad scene in the discotheque, is unreal. But I think sometimes we have to sit back and look at our world: Our world of overindulgence in food and drink and pills; our world of divorce and alienation; our world of the double standards where the youngster will find a mother popping Demerol into her mouth and the father downing Anacin and Compose; the uncle drinking two or three Martinis before dinner: our world with the twin values of "top dog" and "top dollar"; our world which was already addicted to drugs long before the current uproar about LSD or marijuana. Now, since we pride ourselves on being a body politic that pledges allegiance under God, since that is the root of our nation, embedded in the Protestant ethic, and since I am speaking to you as a clergyman, I think it would perhaps serve as well, and I say perhaps, to take a look at or at least touch upon the normal aspect of the drug scene.

I am sure that the question, the "moral question," is a significant one. And here I am using morality, in the traditional sense, as sort of a tool. You know, that we can use an instrument that we can say is wrong or it's right. We can use morality to pry loose a very sensitive situation, or we can use it as a cloak for our own lack of concern or lack of ability in the matter. I don't think we should fall into the trap again of using morality, as sort of, you're-damned-if-you-do-it and you-are-blessed-if-you-don't kind of approach, and let it go at that. Let me just briefly touch on a point or two about the morality of the present situation. I think, first of all, before we point an accusing finger to anyone who uses a pill or any kind of a drug, we should acknowledge the failure of our churches and the failure of traditional ethics to approach the problems of this day and age. I don't think, and I say this with embarrassment, that we as churchmen have really come to grips with the young.

As a very prominent and much respected official here in Riverside said to me just the other day, "Father, in all our discussion about urban renewal, where are the churches?" "Are they in our ghettos, are they helping the people in our slums, are they reaching out to the young, are they helping; where are they?" We find the politicians there, we find the administrators and the educators; where is the church? I think this applies in a very particular way to our youth. I have seen church activities and church services geared for the very, very young—those to be confirmed or those to be Baptized—and for the elders, but very few geared for the young. You know that tremendous gap when a youngster reaches the age of thirteen through the age to twenty-five; they prefer to wipe out the church as a real area of influence in his or her life. And I can say this with some authority because of dealing with it here at the UCR campus and Riverside City College, as a campus chaplain. Perhaps the greatest challenge that comes to the campus minister, or to any campus chaplain of any denomination, is the painful process of "winning back" the dispossessed, the alienated—those that come to us to say "we have had it with the church." They have been forced to go to church or to catechism, they have been plied with the traditional morality that says do this and don't do that, because the book says so, or because I say so with very little reason. To be sure—a few good things are being done. I don't want to be entirely negative here. There are folk masses and folk liturgies; no matter how you feel about these, many of these services are reaching the young people. There is an attempt to sort of "jazz up" if you will, the liturgy, in terms that they will understand the word of God. There is an attempt by some to get young people involved in social action groups, such as the tutorial project here at U.C.R., the Unicamp program and other programs connected, for example, with the Casa Blanca House here at Riverside. There is also an attempt to win back these vast numbers of the dispossessed and alienated youngsters through places like "coffee houses" which are church-oriented. Here the student or the youngster has a chance to voice his own opinions and talk about morality. I think we should make a great appeal to the church to "get with it"— with regard to the young. And what I am saying here is this, that the church cannot really begin to cope with the problems of drugs until it has revitalized itself. I don't think it's fair for the minister or rabbi or clerygman to stand in the pulpit and roundly condemn the young because of their lack of church attendance or because of their use of drugs without rivitalizing his own program for the youth. So I think that just as the drug scene really tells us, and has been telling us this all day; our society is afflicted. But just as it tells us that something is wrong with our society that needs overhauling, perhaps, it tells us that something is wrong with our churches. They are suffering, too.

When we look at the church in this area, I sincerely hope the church-orientated people and religious-minded people have at last learned the first lesson of the Gospel which is that he who is without sin be the first to cast the stone.

I think that finally, for me, speaking as a clergyman again, the real abuse of drugs stems not so much from overindulgence or even from the harmful effects, but rather from what they represent. And I think they often represent things like apathy, defiance, carelessness, and lack of concern either about oneself or about one's neighbor. If a drug represents defiance, if it represents carelessness, then certainly the issue of morality is at stake. But I think if the moral issue is going to be raised along with the medical and legal aspects and the societal, if the moral issue is going to be raised, then raise it on valid moralistic grounds. The moral is not to say how much is wrong. This doesn't work. It seems to me to tell young people, it is wrong to go bad because someone says so or because the good book says so, is to miss the issue. To speak of them and discuss with them and to listen to them about their concerns; about apathy or lack of care, about their needs, about their loneliness, about alienation, about their problems, in so many areas, I think this is to come closer at least to bridging the gap between the moral world of the adult and the ethic of the teenager.

DR. DEMOS: It is true that the young people are fleeing the church and feel as though it does not have the kind of impact that we hoped it would have and until members of the clergy become enlightened, as I feel Father O'Connor is, and other younger clergymen, particularly chaplains of colleges and universities, we are going to have serious difficulties in bringing these youth back. As I listen to them, interestingly enough, Father O'Connor, they are talking about and asking religious questions, moral questions. The drug user refers to his experience with God, with love, and talks about religious experiences. Many of them seem to be almost in an unconscious way searching for some kind of a religious experience through drugs, something they haven't been able to achieve through the traditional church experiences, and perhaps if more of the clergy would become in tune to this kind of need that young people seem to be striving for, the existential questions that Dr. Fisher talked about, too, in terms of "Who am I?" "What is life all about?" "Why am I here?" Moral questions, ethical questions indeed, that are exceedingly difficult questions and we, as educators, have not been very interested in dealing with these questions. We are not able to do so. We feel so inadequate, and we haven't been very innovative educationally, morally, religiously in helping young people come to grips with some of the most pressing problems facing all of us here today.

MR. JAN HORN: We can say some nice things, but I really doubt whether way down deep in our hearts we really want to do anything preventive about this problem. In my contacts with the school psychologists in the Riverside Schools, and I don't have anything against the Riverside Schools, but I think this is typical of many, many institutions because we have a set of standards to maintain, we have to teach the kids what to do right. I don't think that we really want to get to the real crux of the problem because it is going to show us, as Dr. Fisher has said, as lacking. They don't have any respect for us, because when we start talking, they tune us out right away. In the city schools in Riverside, we are getting deluged with films about what to do, and when you try to liken the use of marijuana and playing Russian roulette, they are laughing at you. It is a strain to get just to the end of the movie because the whole class breaks up into pandemonium because they've heard this line so much, and they know it's not true, and even so they like to play the exemption syndrome anyway that if it's going to happen to the next guy it is not going to happen to them.

So in my work, I've been trying to get to the root of the problems and try to work with the kids individually. I have a group of kids, narcotics users, who are meeting regularly, and we don't talk about drugs any more; we are talking about other problems, about families, about alienation with their families and with meaningful adults. They think all teachers are cynics and, they are very ashamed of their parents because either they have been divorced or are drinking or are yelling and screaming at each other all of the time and so, of course, they want to fade out of the scene and get away. But I am interested in specifics because I am in the foxholes of human behavior and when you're in the foxholes, man, you have to come up with stuff or you get shot down pretty quickly, so I've been looking for some specifics, and I have some specifics. We have a discussion group going in one school. We tried it in another school and it was going fabulously until the school district came out with the policy—and I know at least thirty school districts in Southern California have the same policy—as soon as the school counselor hears that a kid is using the stuff, he has to report it to the principal who then reports it to the police and then to the parents. And this is all right from the adult standpoint, but what does it do to the kids? It chops off your contact with the kid immediately.

I had a stream of kids coming to me from one city high school through the counselors, through all sorts of nice channels and it was all open and above board. As soon as the district school policy came out, "whamoo" I haven't had a referral since the beginning of November. I was talking to a kid yesterday from another school and he said, "How can we talk about these things?" How can I say to my counselor, 'I'd like to have a group discussion on narcotics?'" "I can't even bring it up in my classrooom, because as soon as we bring it up my teacher says, 'Aha you're one of those!' And we're in fear of being turned in to the principal."

Now the state law says you may be suspended. I would think that would be under extreme circumstances. We got the word that says that in most cases the normal kid that is suspected of using the stuff—suspected, not proved by the courts—is going to be suspended, or expelled, or something along that line and it completely drives out our contact with the kids. I have to speak to P.T.A. groups. What do you tell parents hopeful that their kids haven't been exposed to this stuff? I asked this group of narcotic kids, "What do you tell a group of parents?" They gave me my whole speech.

The first thing is that from the day the kid is born you should develop a liking relationship with your kid. They don't say love, because you know "smother love" can stamp out a lot of things. Like your kid, keep your level of discussion open, and be frank with your kid. Just accept him as a human individual. Secondly, don't panic and call the cops the first time you feel that he has used drugs. What good does that do? Learn all the facts, parents, so when you find some of the stuff in his pockets, you know you're not going to say that the end of the world is going to come. Thirdly, you want to open up the channels of communication. Whatever you do, don't make the kid promise never to do it again, or you've already estranged him one more time. And whatever you do, don't give up on your kid because kids learn through bad experiences, they say, and this is true. Don't we all learn through bad experiences? Keep the lines of communication open. When do the police come in? It is a matter of morals, breaking the law. Only bring in the police, say these kids, when the kid is totally out of hand and it is a matter of health, and you as a parent don't have any control. But if you go to the law-enforcement people too soon you are giving up the responsibilities that you as a parent have. And the kid knows this and then he doesn't have any respect for you. These are the down-to-earth, common-sense kinds of things that these kids are bringing up if you just provide a climate where they can express themselves.

MR. SHARP: "Basic knowledge is lacking about the causes of drug abuse. The largest gap in our present knowledge has to do with the drug abuser as a human being in the family and in the community. Knowledge of proper treatment and rehabilitation procedures is sadly lacking." These were comments from the final report of the President's Advisory Commission on Narcotics and Drug Abuse in November, 1963. The President's Commission found that public and professional education in this field was inadequate. They found the problem clouded by misconceptions and distorted by persistent fallacies. Unfortunately, these conclusions are as valid to date as they were then. Misinformation about drugs and their effects is still prevalent and the measures taken by the Federal Government to correct the misinformation is still limited and fragmented. We still are suffering from this same dilemma, obviously. We still don't have the answers. The suggestions that Mr. Van Horn gives us and those we heard this morning are excellent, and what we are doing here today, I think is a step in the right direction toward resolving some of these problems.

We attempt sometimes to lay at the door of social phenomenon the responsibility for drug abuse. Sociologists say it's a matter of a cultural phenomenon; psychologists say perhaps it's a psychological phenomenon. We've even asked physicians to determine whether or not it is a physiological phenomenon. We often observe, for example, that the protestant ethic has been abandoned nationally. And we say a lot of things that sound good that may be partially true, but they aren't the total answer to what we're trying to resolve.

I represent a public agency, the probation department. We are charged with the responsibility of finding ways to help kids that are in trouble. We don't have the answer, in the probation department in the juvenile court, to drug use. Our approach to this whole drug abuse problem when a youngster is referred to us from a school, from law enforcement, or from parents, is to approach the matter of treatment on the basis of the individual case as it comes to us. We just recently, as Mr. Van Horn commented this morning, have acquired a delinquency prevention officer we feel will be helpful in getting out into the communities and setting up programs and discussing with parents the problems of drug abuse. We feel this prevention is necessary and something that we haven't had before. We're involved with the P.T.A. this year and with Sheriff Clark's office in going out into each P.T.A. unit in the county and in the district with a film and a program on Narcotics and Drug abuse. We're trying to reach the parent.

We became aware some time ago that parents are figuratively "in the middle." The youngsters are getting drug abuse education in the schools, the teachers are being furnished with manuals that give some very valid and very good information on drug abuse, and the parents sit out there in an informational void; and it isn't infrequent that we get calls from parents saying. "Gee, I found some pills in my youngsters' trouser pocket this morning when I put them in the wash. My youngster was up all night, and he didn't seem to be able to sleep and his eyes were dilated. What does marijauna smell like? What do these drugs look like? How do the youngsters behave and with whom do they associate, etc.?" And, again the public is confused about the notions on narcotics and drug abuse. It is a new phenomenon.

You will recall that as recently as ten years ago the youngster that used marijuana was, for the most part, of a minority ethnic group of youngsters that, perhaps as a subcultural thing, began to use marijuana; and our penalties were strong and our measures of dealing with them in juvenile courts were strict. It was not, as it is becoming now, a middle-class problem. I think that we're not as strict in the juvenile courts now as we used to be. Again, perhaps partially because we are intimidated by the phenomenon and we don't really understand it.

These comments have indicated some of the things that we're doing as a public agency, and I would move that the

National Institute of Mental Health or the Rosenberg Foundation, or some such institution, pour money into the study of the total phenomenon of drug use in society today—so that we can build some research around us as we go along, so that we can develop knowledge and techniques for dealing with prevention and treatment of drug abuse.

Mrs. Weiner: We've had a very successful program at the Desert Sands Unified School District where we took a young man just out of college. He took over a class of youngsters who had been in trouble and were involved with narcotics. He reaches these youngsters and does it very well. He knows their way of talking; he understands their problems and he teaches them and he inspires them, and he has led a great many of them out of this morass, which was the result of other problems in their home lives and their social lives. This young man has reached these youngsters, and I think has probably succeeeded in rehabilitating more in the short time that he has been involved with them than any of us of the older generations who are turned off. I think perhaps this may be our solution. Let some of our young people who understand and comprehend and are a part of the generation experiencing this upheaval, talk and be involved with the problems and let them guide the youngsters out of it.

Dr. Demos: Along that same line, we have had an experience on our campus with a most effective drug-abuse educational program which I think can go to other schools as well. It's in our experimental college, along the same line, in which the student himself decides on the curriculum. They pick the speakers; they bring the resources that they wish to hear; and they bring users, former users; those who are clean, law-enforcement people, etc. The students run the program and we have had a course on drug education in our experimental college in which no credit is given. We can't get a course of this kind approved through our curriculum committee so we merely provide the facilities on our campus so that young people can bring courses that they want to study. We have one course now entitled "Drugs, Sex, and Values" which is also a very important topic and in which large numbers of students are interested, and they themselves bring their own resources. They talk about their own experiences, the same kind of things we have been discussing.

Mr. ROGER HARLOW:I think we're still looking for a simple answer and have concluded by now that there isn't any. And there isn't one answer, at least I can't see how one answer can solve the problems that were just mentioned. I'm a parent and my children are all Junior High School age age or younger, and they haven't started using drugs, obviously. I'm working with high-school kids on the one hand who are already using it, and the solution to the problem of preventing my children or younger children from using it is a different one from what do we do with the one who is.

I find myself divided in discussions here. I am working in what I consider a counseling kind of a role, and on the other hand I carry in my pocket a card that has Sheriff Clark's autograph on it which indicates that I am a special deputy in the sheriff's office. I may give the card back to Sheriff Clark any day now, in order to clarify my own personal feelings about this. I don't use it often. I think in eight or nine years I've used it once or twice to impress somebody that I have a certain amount of authority.

My concern is that we have an immediate problem. I see in the audience here probation officers with whom I work almost daily, and they have people in their case book who are already using drugs and have been through court. They are attempting with the help of the schools to get the problem solved. We have in our minds a backlog of cases not yet brought to their attention, and we know that they exist.

My function is to serve as liaison to these people and at the same time try to convince kids that these are human beings, these probation officers and deputy sheriffs and police officers are trying to help them just as much as the counselor, the psychologist, the administrator and the teacher. And if I can do anything here to bring us all together, I don't like the idea that Sheriff Clark is heading a bunch of punitive people here because I think they are not. I don't like to think of Mr. Sharp or Mr. Jan Horn, or Mr. Jeffrey, or Mr. Williams, or all the people that I have dealt with in the probation department are punitive either. I think they are all counselors and I think that to simplify my statement here to look for one answer or consult one person is futile. To look for one person to do it in any community is also futile. Each one has to go back and do his part.

QUESTIONS AND ANSWERS

QUESTION: I might add one approach which has been used in our community with an attempt to solve a problem—but I can only say that it has created further problems for the school—and that is that the press in our community, a local daily, adopted the policy of printing the names and addresses of students and parents when an arrest is made regarding narcotics or dangerous drug problems. This immediately then puts the knowledge of who is involved in the hands of every parent and throws immediately upon the school the problem of what should be done at that point in the school system.

DR. DEMOS: I would like to speak against that policy. I feel that is a punitive policy that clearly adds to the problem in terms of the embarrassment of the family, and concern for the youngster involved. I think that this kind of action is something that one would expect back in the middle ages, but I can't see anything very therapeutic about it. I would speak out very strongly in opposing this kind of harrassment and embarrassment to the family involved, and the youngster involved. I hope that some action is taken to alleviate this practice.

QUESTION FROM AUDIENCE: Dr. Demos, you mentioned this experimental class that was quite effective, and in a measure how do we know it is effective?

DR. DEMOS: Yes, this is a very good point. We don't know really how effective it is. We haven't done that kind of research. We are not researchers, and I encourage all of you to do research in this area because it is so direly needed. The only thing I can say is that the young people who have these sessions seem to leave and feel as though they are getting something out of it.

They're not tuning out some of the old "V.D." type movies, the old comic book approach which occasionally you see distributed. Many young people will tune this out and turn it off. It just doesn't reach many of them. Now, there is an occasional film and book that will, but this a human approach—an approach in which we're not afraid to look at all sides. Those who encourage the use of drugs, and those who have been drug users and now resort to other means, whether it be religion, medication, or fresh air and the outdoors—many are turning over to a new kind of commitment, finding something else in which they can invest themselves without the use of potentially dangerous drugs.

SHERIFF CLARK: I'll tell you what I think the schools could do, and I'll tell you what I think law enforcement is going to do. As far as we can see, there is a necessity for the teacher to understand some of the medical things that have been discussed. We feel that as a department, and I should be talking about law enforcement in general, we'll involve ourselves in any way, shape or form with the schools, or with the parents to make them aware through participation in this education program. We also feel that there is a law, and that this law is based on facts from medical authorities who have told us why there should or should not be regulations of narcotics. We recognize the fact that there is a need for order in society and in this instance relates to the abuse of narcotics. We'll enforce the laws and help provide order. We recognize also that there is a punishment connected with the misuse of drugs and narcotics. To have order you must have stringent enforcement, surety of apprehension, swift prosecution, and fair treatment under the law. As to stringent enforcement, I'd reemphasize as I did this morning that there is no fear, or should be no fear that every time an individual calls a police agency that the only thing they are interested in is in making an arrest. We recognize that we're working with all society, that there are things which change. We are supposed to represent society, and just so that you're not confused, law enforcement will enforce existing laws, until society as a group tells us, "We as a society want you, the police, to take a new approach by law."

FATHER O'CONNOR: I think that there is nothing wrong in saying that each one of us who came here today came to be informed and committed and dedicated, and I hope your words don't imply that the police officer is the only one that has to make a decision after today. The educator, the priest, the counselor who talks to a user, or users, day in and day out—each one has to make constant decisions as to whether to call the police and how to help in the situation. And I think all of us, I would hope, are concerned about the problem and have to make a decision. What are we, individually, going to do about it from hereon. I think we have become enlightened on the matter with regard to the law. I do hope we have become committed, because each one of us has people that we're committed to. Whether or not they use drugs, or whether or not they are simply alienated or lonely, or are children—they need help; if we are not somehow committed, admitting honestly our own confusion but still dedicated to the problem, then we have the wrong motives in the first place and we shouldn't even be here.

PART IV
STUDENT REACTION PANEL TO DRUG ABUSE

IT SHOULD BE STATED that various school districts in Riverside County selected the Student Reaction Panel. As a protection to each student panel member selected, to his or her parents, to school district and community, it was decided to avoid selecting a student panel representative of the drug problem. While a representative panel may have added some dimensions of meaning and direct communication to the symposium, it could have presented some legal problems. Thus, the students were selected for their interest and participation in school and community activities. We believe you will find that the student panel did an excellent job in reacting to the symposium and in expressing their own opinions about the drug problem among youth.

DR. SLAUGHTER (MODERATOR): Now you've already met three of these people several times today, but most of the people on this panel on my left you have not met: Eric Asker, Desert Sands Unified School; Christey Hayes, Beaumont School; Arthur Torres, Desert Sands; Eileen Stuve, Alvord; Scott Anderson, Palm Springs; William Terry, Beaumont; Cammy Larson, Palm Springs; Jerry Maio, Alvord. All right, panelists, you've listened to us all day. What are your reactions at this point? What do you think about the fact that while we were having lunch, probably a ton of marijuana was sold in the high-school parking lots of this area.

YOUNG LADY: First of all I'd like to say that I think your program has been very informative and interesting, but personally as a student at the high school I attend, we don't have that much traffic in mariquana or LSD or anything like that, so it's very difficult for us to give our opinions on this as far as what you can do to help the individual because we are not directly involved as we are not taking these narcotics. But I personally think that a lot of the problem stems from the fact that the students do have personal problems and personal pressures from

61

society. A lot of thought is put on the fact that they must succeed in life, that they must do something, have to be someone, they have to find themselves. And I don't know whether this is directly the parent's fault or who is at fault, but I think there needs to be an understanding between the adults and the youth.

DR. SLAUGHTER: Other reactions.

YOUNG LADY: I thought that Dr. Fisher was excellent in his speech but there is one question. Where and who is the person that the kids can turn to? If they go to a counselor at school, it's all over school and all of the kids know that they have gone to this counselor. If they go to their parents, the parents jump on the kids and they say you're not that mixed up, you're just having regular teenage problems. And some of the kids really are mixed up and they need the help. They are afraid and they don't know what they want or who to turn to. They need someone to talk to and to explain things to. But there is no one to listen, no one that can really understand what they're talking about, so these kids say that they just can't accept reality, I've got to use something else to help me accept it so they go to the drug. And this I feel is a big mistake and if there were only someone that the kids could talk to without having any fear of being talked down or misunderstood, but just someone to sit and listen. I think this would help a great deal.

DR. SLAUGHTER: Thank you. Dr. Fisher, would you like to react to that?

DR. FISHER: I feel she is pointing out how kids are desperate for real human communication. Who is there when you really have something you want to talk about? You say you can't talk to the parents. Someone is concerned about the counselors because they might have to turn in the drug user or because other kids would know. I'm curious. Are there certain teachers or other people that you know are available? Is this a general problem which you are in agreement on?

YOUNG LADY: I disagree. I think that if I had a problem like this, I don't think I'd ever have a problem like this, but I can talk to my parents. That's why I wouldn't have a problem. I know a lot of persons here in town you could talk to. I think you could even talk to some of the counselors around, maybe not all of them, and even a few of the teachers. I can think of a lot of clergymen around, especially the younger clergymen. You go and talk to them and they'll discuss it with you.

MODERATOR: Are young people talking? Are they searching out clergymen to talk to or are they going along just having this feeling of frustration?

YOUNG MAN: Most of them want to stay to themselves. They get on drugs or something and they're with themselves. They don't care enough really to go down to see a clergyman or one of the teachers or counselors. They really don't know where to go because of the fear of being turned in. Some of them just don't care really. They haven't got good home relations or anything else and they don't care what happens to them. They've just sort of given up.

YOUNG LADY: They have their own little group of kids that do it and they do it and don't include anybody else in this little circle. I can't talk to some of the kids either. I usually don't know who it is that is using it. I really haven't had too much association with people who do it, but I heard of a few people and we're in different worlds—you can't talk to them.

YOUNG MAN: Listening to all the panel, I feel the complete responsibility lies on the users as teenagers. I would think the biggest problem is at home with the parent—that the parent doesn't take that much interest; they don't know that much about it to help us or the ones that are using it. There should be some plan or some way of teaching parents and adults more about narcotics.

YOUNG MAN: Well, I know this one boy says he uses LSD at school and that when he talks about it these other students build it up, glorifying it like it's something great. They look for it to relieve their problems, and they kind of build it up and they look for somebody that does it. It gives them an attitude that it is okay, and I think, well, our standards have almost made this acceptable. I feel that it is not only the student's or the person's fault, but it is the whole society's problem.

YOUNG MAN: I also think it is unfortunate that you picked

us in some ways because we are not representative of the drug user's crowd. Also, I think it will probably shock most of the adults here, but I think a growing segment of the younger population has discarded certain established ethics and that the drugs have become a way of life and they feel it is an individual decision, and it should not be regulated by law. A couple of months ago I remember hearing about a lady principal of an elementary school in Northern California. She was a pillar of her community, and she came to the defense of someone who was smoking marijuana and explained that she had been on pot for at least fifteen years. I think it's for better or for worse the law exists and I can sympathize with Sheriff Clark, because I know that many times the hands of the law officers are tied.

MAN: (from audience): The point has been made, and I think it has not been made here before today, and perhaps it should have been as it has been implied here. We're really talking about two different populations entirely. You talk about one population which is the small hard core, not criminal, or whatever you want to call it, and that's one little group that might also be narcotics addicts of one kind or another. Then you have another large group of people who occasionally, indulge in some form of drug consumption and apparently, according to the figures cited, an increasingly large segment of the youth population belongs to this group. Yet, we have one set of laws that apply to both groups, the tough group that has always been a tough group to deal with and the occasional user group.

YOUNG LADY: I don't think that I can ever as yet think two sets of laws. Obviously we have these two different types of people, but this college kid is just experimenting. A lot of times I've met kids who've said I've been thinking of taking pot, with a roommate, you know the hippie type that keeps talking about taking pot. It's not very harmful, they say. Drinking is more harmful than pot. Smoking is more harmful. Drinking becomes quite violent at times, but with pot you're very peaceful. You just sit in a corner and see pretty colors. This is their thinking that they go through and they don't really see anything wrong with it. They just want to try it the same as everybody else is doing.

YOUNG MAN: They go out one night, booze it up and have fun and then they drop it and with nothing else to do, they go out and get some pot and smoke for awhile. They have fun that night, then they go home, sleep a long time and get up. It's all gone. They're just regular students, and they go out the next night and get drunk and if they don't feel like it they don't smoke. They want to have some fun and haven't done it before so they do it for fun and think it's not going to hurt them. Why not do it for one night. All of a sudden they're doing it regularly. They just think about it for one night; they don't think about the future.

MODERATOR: They don't think about the future?

YOUNG MAN: Not usually I've heard. The kids around school just think of one night.

MODERATOR: Have these youngsters you're describing ever been exposed to any films or lectures or discussions or anything dealing with this area?

YOUNG MAN: Not at our school. I think we've had one or two films but they haven't been on drugs.

YOUNG MAN: We had something at our school last year like that but the public seemed to be against it. It seemed like everybody was against the idea of teaching sex or anything about drugs or marijuana or anything like that. I think that is one reason why we should try to teach the public first.

MODERATOR: There was no public support for an educational program?

YOUNG LADY: I was going to say that setting up two sets of laws, using just one part of the time is going to get you into trouble because you're just inviting those students who have never participated to go ahead and start in with marijuana or something like this because they know they're not going to be in trouble, or maybe won't ever get caught, but the second time maybe they still won't get caught. By the time they get caught, they may have already tried it several times and may be addicted by then. Then the charges are going to be less and they'll get off easier, and then they can just get right back into it.

YOUNG MAN: On the other hand, there is the old saying that you can't legislate morality. It seems to me the strictness of the law isn't going to have any effect on people who want to do something.

YOUNG LADY: I think that if we were better informed about drugs, it would help. Many of us have talked to each other about the problem and have discussed the problem, but is there any way that we can possibly get a group of these men, one or two on each of these topics to go around to all of the schools in the district, or as many as possible and talk to the kids and try to explain to them what we've heard here today? I think it would be an excellent idea and it might help, even if it just kept one of the kids off dope—I think it would be worth it and I think you could probably get more than just one.

MODERATOR: It was mentioned that a growing number of our young people are disenchanted with the protestant ethic, and I'm intrigued to know what your view is on this—if our young people are disallowing the standards and values of the older generation. Is this number increasing to such an extent that this will become the new ethic or which ethic is going to win?

YOUNG MAN: I think that the new morality, or whatever you want to call it, is going to continue to gain supporters, but I think there are enough of us "solid Americans" who are going to continue the same morality that has been handed down to us.

MODERATOR: One of your panel said that the students were afraid to go to their counselors or to the people involved in education. I'd like to know where the breakdown is—where education can take a look at itself and say—we've slipped. What can we do now to help these students?

YOUNG LADY: Well, the thing you need is someone that is close to our own age but who is older and wiser and can listen to these kids and understand their problems without repeating them. Because if you can get one person who has the trust of the kids, if he can get that trust, then he can do a world of good.

But if you don't have the trust, then it's all lost.

MODERATOR: I might add that that is one thing that has come up over and over today. The significance of an objective counselor, whatever special type that person happens to be, whether a teacher, a counselor, a probation officer or policeman.

MAN: (from audience) I think the trust is there. I think the trouble here is your communication with us. We're on a different level. We're a generation older. We don't understand the lingo, and consequently kids won't talk to their parents because their parents are old-fashioned. People won't talk to their counselor because their counselor is old-fashioned.

YOUNG MAN: The reason I think a lot of high-school students and junior high-school students don't want to talk to the older generation is because they don't understand. I try to talk to my parents about narcotics, but I think I know more about it than they do right now.

MAN: (from audience) Don't you think there is an active difference between listening and hearing? Maybe this is what some of us adults are doing, hearing and not listening and speaking but really not communicating.

MODERATOR: I might just throw this general question out to the students to get their reaction. You've heard Dr. Demos explain about the students at Long Beach State College. How do you feel about the possible success of asking your folks and your peers, who you want to hear, rather than adults deciding that we're going to have Dr. Demos out, or Dr. Fisher, or some other old-fashioned person to tell you what we think you ought to hear. Can we successfully approach it through this point of view?

YOUNG LADY: I don't think it matters how old the person is that we hear or what his name is or anything like that as long as he isn't afraid to speak about the younger generation and really doesn't feel that there is that much of a bridge or a gap between the two generations. I personally don't feel that there is that much of a gap if we focus on similarities rather than differences. I mean that we're all people and we all have something to say. I think that is all we want—someone who will listen to us.

YOUNG LADY: I just wanted to say that it sounds like it is a good idea and I suppose it would go over well as a good start if you had students who were capable of conveying their ideas. I don't know how well I could go to students, and there are a very few in our school who could do it, and explain to them the defects and harm of taking narcotics. Now for me personally, it's affected me very strongly, but it is difficult for me to convey my ideas, so I don't know how much good I'd be.

DR. DEMOS: First of all I would like to make a point. I don't want you to get the impression that something is necessarily wrong with the drug user, that he is a different kind of an animal so to speak. Many of the drug users, generally at the college level, are intelligent, sensitive, caring individuals. I think you would be absolutely amazed to find out the energy of some of the young people who have tried a variety of drugs. And I also agree that we are unfortunate that we don't have with us today some of the proponents of drugs from the student point of view. I think perhaps that would have been an eye opener for all of us, for all of you who haven't had this opportunity to see that many of them are exceedingly articulate and have very good reasons for some of their usages of drugs.

This is a pretty musty approach we've used with these young people. It simply doesn't work. They turn us off and tune us out, and there are some with whom it doesn't work, I grant you. In the main, I think, the young people here have also stated something that has been stated by several other people. Somewhere along the line we have a communication gap. We're not talking the same language; we're not communicating. Certain people mentioned that Dr. Fisher got through to them. There are certain people, regardless of their age, who do seem to get through to young people, whether they be high school students or college students. I think we need to reach and search out these people and cherish them and work with them and put them in positions where they can continue to work with young people without the fear of being chastised or criticized by the local community, the police, the board, etc.

There are many individuals who are fearful of doing this for fear of what kind of results will happen, the kind of publicity that is sometimes associated with drugs. We did a research study on our campus. Just to show you the kind of publicity and how it can be misinterpreted, and be sensationalized, the press got hold of this. They happened to pick out one incident of the entire study, and the incident they picked out made a blazing headline. The headline was this—50% of the students of California State College at Long Beach use illicit drugs. Let me tell you exactly what we found. We found that approximately 50 percent of our students had tried at least one drug without medical advice, whether that be a tranquilizer at one time or another, methedrine, a pep pill, a diet pill, etc. A very small percentage of our students had used marijuana at least once, 4 percent had tried LSD at that time. But this is the sensationalism that sometimes is associated with this whole drug movement, and as a result of this, it has frightened a lot of individuals who have the kind of skills that these young people are looking for and fear that they are going to be labeled, they're going to be chastised and criticized very harshly.

It behooves all of you in administrative positions to protect individuals who have the kinds of skills and can communicate and reach young people. We desperately need them at all levels, not just at the high-school level. We desperately need them at the college level, and most of us are really not able to communicate in this fashion. It takes a special aptitude and ability to really talk their lingo, to really communicate. And when we find this kind of ability by all means we have to utilize it and put it to use wherever it is.

I think we can talk about laws, talk about educational programs, and talk about many diverse programs and all of these need to be available. We have to work on a multidimensional approach and multidisciplinary approach. We have to bring together the police and the rest of the law-enforcement people, the psychiatrists, the medical profession, the pharmaceutical people, the parents and the housewife, and somehow those people who can communicate with kids. There happens to be a woman who runs a taco stand across from a ghetto high school in Los Angeles who can communicate with kids like no one in the high school has ever been able to communicate with kids. You know what they did? She doesn't have an eighth-grade education. They hired her. She is now working as a teacher aide. This is the kind of person we need to recruit and solicit because we haven't been innovative in many of the approaches we've used when the creative minority in a society, to use Toynbee's words, become the dominant minority, it ceases to innovate in favor of protecting the status quo. Then it must expect attack and rebellion from the disenfranchised portion of society, and this is precisely what we have in the drug situation at present.

DR. FISHER: These students are telling us they want to talk with someone who will listen and try to understand. They want a trusting relationship; however, I can't conceive of this kind of relationship existing if the fear of "being turned in" is present. As a psychiatrist I can't imagine working with students if I felt an obligation to "turn anyone in." I can say that at U.C.L.A. I've never been asked by any law-enforcement agency or anyone else to turn anyone in.

I don't see how a counselor could work with young people if he felt that kind of a double obligation. It would be very difficult for me. I also think that many of the answers, or part of the answers, come from the young people themselves. For one thing, the fact that the two generations are together here is something. I find it very rewarding. I attend so many P.T.A. meetings where angry parents and teachers say it's terrible, it's awful, and we all leave feeling relieved, but the young people being discussed are not there. Whatever happened to them? *I think meetings like this and further meetings with young people involved would be extremely helpful.* I think approaches which enable someone who really cares or is concerned to get exposure to young people will be helpful.

Once I spoke at a military school where the kids were mostly from divorced homes and families with problems. Most of them were upper middle class. When I walked into that school I went to the principal's office and met the prototype of the archconservative headmaster with a white moustache, however, his attitude was very different. He said, "Arrange the presentation any way you want to, but I want the kids to know about drugs." As I spoke to the students, I watched them react to him. Beneath his miltary attitude was a man who was really concerned about every student in that school. He knew them by name; he was strict and had them sit in a very military way, but they liked him because his feeling self was evident. He really cared about them.

When I met with the students informally, they said, "You know he's really tough; he makes us get up at six thirty in the morning and makes us get squared away." It wasn't his rigidity or the fact that he enforced rules, but his *concern about everyone of them that counted. He was concerned enough to bring in speakers and try new approaches.* And I think here is one of the answers. Help young people have the opportunity to be with people who are really interested and want to understand!

DR. DEMOS: Those of you who are familiar with the basic encounter groups will know that this is also very effective in bringing the segments of the population together. Get your young people together for periodic meetings in which they can confront each other. Bring your administrators, a board member, police officer, user and nonusers all together for sessions, in-depth sessions in which they can really confront each other on issues and bring this gap that we all talk about down to a real discussion level. I think that if you can get more of these groups going it will be an education for all parties, including the young people, who can then have a better understanding of why we are the way we are, why we're materialistically orientated, what makes us tick.

SECTION TWO
WHAT PROGRESS IS BEING MADE? IMPLICATIONS FOR A NEW APPROACH TO EDUCATION

CONTRIBUTORS

Herbert O. Brayer
Coronado Unified School District
Coronado, California

James C. Bennett, ED.D.
California State College
Fullerton, California

Thomas A. Shannon
Schools' Attorney
San Diego Unified School District
  and
Legal Counsel
California Association of School
  Administrators

George D. Demos, Ph.D.
California State College
Long Beach, California

John W. Shainline
Assistant Dean of Students
California State College
Long Beach, California

Allen Y. Cohen, Ph.D.
John F. Kennedy University
Martinez, California

AN OVERVIEW OF WHAT IS BEING DONE

Herbert O. Brayer

So RAPIDLY HAS THE drug problem grown in the months be-tween our symposium and this publication of its reports that a brief review of developments in this field is desirable. The problem has spread rapidly from college drug abuse to an epi-demic involvement of high-school and junior high-school stu-dents (not just in California, but throughout the nation—and in-deed in many foreign lands). Frightening are the undeniably authentic reports of creeping involvement in the grade or ele-mentary schools with reports showing some youngsters as far down as the third grade being involved with marijauna and "pill taking." In one Southern California county, seven deaths among teenagers and subteenagers occurred due to sniffing glue, in-haling the powerful fumes from a variety of aerosol products and using other dangerous substances. Surveys continue to in-dicate that more and more children are risking health and even life through misuse and abuse of drugs, narcotics and dangerous substances that are readily obtainable—many from their own home kitchens, bathrooms or parents' dressing tables.

Throughout California (and many other states from coast to coast, including both Hawaii and Alaska where the problem is already a serious one) public and private school officials—ele-mentary and secondary—have endeavored to meet the situation in a variety of ways. Scores of crash education programs have been undertaken—mostly with different results; a number of in-depth curriculum programs have been implemented and some of these are beginning to show areas wherein progress in drug misuse *prevention* may become effective. Unfortunately, much effort this past year has been expended in trying to develop a traditional approach rather than to seek innovative and mo-tivating solutions which will have more promise of effective-

76

ness. Our decades of failure in curbing both tobacco and alcohol use through education seems to have taught us very little.

Some very positive and promising steps have been taken in the preventive drug education field. First, the State of California has implemented under Dr. Angela Kitzinger and Miss Pat Hill a statewide study of the school-age drug-abuse based problem with the end of developing a suggested curriculum based on the results of many programs already being developed by school districts and counties. This program is now well into its second year and materials of significance to the schools should be available during the 1970-71 school year.

A wide range of commercial anti-drug-abuse education programs are now available to educators. Among these are the 3M Company Health Education program highlighting the entire drug-abuse problem, the newly tested multi-media Lockheed "Crisis" approach program designed to motivate students at both the elementary and secondary levels, the Raytheon sound film program, Tane Press' "Tell It as It Is" programmed learning series and the familiar SVE "Drugs in Our Society" to name but a few in use in various California schools. San Francisco schools are implementing a systemwide program using one of these new in-depth programs. Similarly, Pasadena and the Vista school districts are also trying the commercial programs along with their own teacher-developed approaches.

Many schools, districts and counties in California have prepared course studies and unit programs and some of these are well along in testing and implementation. The Los Angeles City School District, under Dr. Joseph Langan, has an in-depth drug abuse project which includes detailed course outlines, films and other student involvement techniques. The San Diego schools have implemented and are expanding programs tuned to the drug problem in both junior and senior high-schools. Other systems with developed programs (including printed curricula), largely along traditional paths include the South Bay (San Diego) Union School District, the Alameda County School Departments, Orange County Schools, Santa Clara County Schools,

Saratoga Elementary School District, San Bernardino County Schools, to name just a few.

Innovative approaches still in their beginning stages are found in a number of areas. The Palos Verdes high schools are developing a curriculum approach to augment a community-wide plan. Los Angeles has implemented "Project Quest." Pasadena City Schools are engaged in a broad multi-media approach using television. Fort Bragg has taken a page from Synanon and is using trained ex-addicts and a "half-way house" to meet an acute problem. Palo Alto has developed a curriculum approach combined with a counseling center using a wide range of professionals and group involvement. Coronado has completed its in-depth study of the problem and is now engaged in putting together a K-12 curriculum approach—directed at student values, responsibility and decision-making—which uses broad student involvement. Other strategies are in various stages of development and implementation in communities and school districts throughout Southern California. From all of this one fact is becoming clearly evident: There is as yet no single successful approach to the drug-abuse problem; it will require considerable time, expense and personnel to ultimately put together the bits and pieces that prove effective in various areas and to adapt them to meet the situations in each geographical area—and then these will require further refinement and constant revision to meet local socioeconomic situations (and, unfortunately, political idiosyncrasies).

One of the more promising developments during the past year has been the realization in a number of communities that drug abuse is more than a police problem; that penal solutions have been even less effective in this area than in the alcohol field during and since prohibition! The astonishing increase in teenage and subteenage drug involvement during the past year has caused anguished pleas from law-enforcement authorities to the schools and the communities "to do something." Numerous communities throughout the state have developed communitywide committees composed of economic, political, social and religious leaders—with strong parent and professional (educational and medical) representation—to take specific action to meet the pressing problems of youth involvement, including drug-abuse prevention.

This involvement of the community and parents augurs well for the development of sound educational approaches. No drug-abuse programs are going to attain real success until the adult world becomes thoroughly involved. Basically, as most authorities in the field have emphatically pointed out, the drug abuse problem among teenagers is symptomatic of much deeper problems that can be resolved only in the home and community. So numerous are these communitywide committees or councils becoming that it is not possible to list them here.

Another development of significance is the active study and action programs being taken in many of California's (and other states') institutions of higher learning. In addition to the programs at the University of California Medical School's Haight-Ashbury Clinic in San Francisco, under Dr. David Smith, there is the excellent program started by Dr. Tom Ungerleider and known as DARE—Drug Abuse Research and Education—Services at the Neuropsychiatric Institute at UCLA. The clinic approach at the California State College at Long Beach under Dr. George Demos and his colleagues is but one of several such programs already doing excellent work at other state educational institutions. In cooperation with a number of adjacent school districts Cerritos College has set up a task force to develop and implement a drug abuse program for schools called "Impact Plus Two."

Professionally directed privately operated nonprofit small group programs are rapidly expanding throughout this state (and, indeed, in many other states such as New York, Connecticut, Texas, Wisconsin, Minnesota, Iowa, Oregon and Washington). These use many techniques including Sensitivity, Encounter and Confrontation. Others are developing techniques that avoid some of the problems found in these psychological approaches. Particular attention is due DAWN (Developing Adolescents Without Narcotics) established in Los Angeles by a dedicated group of high-school teachers, counselors and advanced graduate students led by Mr. Caldwell Williams and Mr. Jordan Paul. In San Diego, Dr. James Kleckner of California Western University has established a small group clinic approach which he also has named DARE. The newly established program for high school and other teenagers involved in drugs set up by the San Diego YMCA under Mrs. Peg Pleskunas and involving the now familiar—and widely used—telephone "hot line" to competent assistance, plus small group therapy is also worthy of note. Similar programs are under consideration or already in operation in other communities.

There has been a considerable advance in the approach of law enforcement agencies toward the drug problem this last year. The California Assembly modified the penalties for marijuana possession and use to give judges the discretion of treating a "first time offender" as guilty of a misdemeanor rather than a felony. Alert police and sheriff's departments have instituted their own educational drug-abuse programs and sought ways to help involved young people without the necessity of being "busted." Probation departments have also gotten into the act with progressive educational programs—sometimes sponsored jointly with the juvenile court justices. A particularly timely and promising program is that established by Judge Richard Vaughn of San Diego County's juvenile court. Selected first time offenders, instead of being otherwise penalized, are put on probation provided they and their parents agree to attend regularly a weekly series of small group sessions established by the county juvenile probation department. Mr. William Sergent is directing the program which includes authoritative presentations of the drug problem followed by group discussions under competent counselors. The program also makes effective use of trained ex-addicts.

It would be remiss to leave out of this all-too-brief and incomplete summary the role being played by media in trying to solve the drug abuse problem among young people. Educational television in Los Angeles, San Francisco and San Diego have produced an astounding array of documentary and panel shows which have been telecast in prime time. While some of these have certainly been controversial, they have served to highlight the problem to many millions of people in this state who otherwise would have been almost totally ignorant of the situation. The newspapers throughout California have run a number of very authoritatively prepared series and articles on the drug problem. One series has been reprinted in booklet form for parents, and is being widely cited. Popular magazine articles on the subject are now so numerous that it is not possible to list them. Worthy of special note, however, are the scores of authoritative articles published in the medical journals throughout this nation. Many of these can be found in the libraries of medical schools and in those of medical societies in almost every major county. To the educator who wants immediate access to these scientific reports—ideal for information as well as for classroom teaching and group discussion, they may be obtained through annual subscription to *Medical Abstract Services for Schools,* O. E. Byrd, M.D., Ed.D., Director, P.O. Box 3721, Stanford, California 94305.

Anyone seeking information on developments in this field should also keep apprised of state developments by contacting Dr. Angela Kitzinger, State Department of Education, 1320 K Street, Sacramento, California 95814. National developments are more difficult to follow, but it is recommended that you follow the work and reports of the National Coordinating Council on Drug Abuse Education and Information, P.O. Box 19400, Washington, D. C. 20036.

ARE WE HELPING TO CREATE A "MONSTER"?

James C. Bennett, ED.D.

Long hair, beards, nonconforming dress and behavior, non-acceptance of adult values and standards—what kind of a "monster" is the younger generation becoming? How did they get this way? What are the factors which have caused them to become such a problem to our adult society?

As members of SMOG ("Smug middle-class older generation") have we considered whether we are, in fact, helping to create the "monster"? Business interests, especially advertising, music and clothing have exploited the younger generation for profit. Three-fourths of the phonograph records and musical equipment sold are purchased by young people. The music world creates teenie-bopper idols and pays them fantastic sums for their services. Charge accounts and easy credit facilitate teenage buying, which has become a multibillion dollar market.

In many homes youth are caught in the middle by the manipulative "Berne-type games" their parents play. Many are pressured by parents to get the "good grades" which lead to college and the security of a middle-class life. Most communities do little in the way of providing youth with adequate outlets for social, emotional, intellectual and physical growth. When teenagers seek their own outlets, they often meet resistance, and at times anger and resentment from the adult community.

Such examples of disinterest or exploitation have led to serious distortions in the value systems of our younger generation. As they observe us in hypocritical political, economic, social and personal interactions, some of our more perceptive youth reject our standards and culture. We, in turn, react defensively instead of trying to understand our contributions to the situation. Teenagers then turn to dissident groups for leadership. Some of the more vital become active leaders in this rebellion and develop followings. They question whether our value system represents a life style worth emulating. The questioning and rejecting may run the gamut from family mores, school and community attitudes, governmental leadership, the economic and military complex, and "The Establishment" in general.

If comfort is needed, we can look to the statements of authorities who declare that the large majority of our youth are conformists, who are passing through this stage with minimal questioning of our values and standards. These young people we can understand. With the others, the battle lines are drawn. Neither side is willing to listen. Both sides "turn off" when an attempt is made to establish communication. One thing is certain: the young rebels will not accept the equivocations of our value system as a model for their lives. They fail (as we "adults" all too frequently do) to recognize the intrinsic worth and validity of the human values system and confuse our lip-service as proving that the values are the faulty element. For our part we revert to an offensive defense (confusing or denying our obvious values deficiencies) and condemn youth for their attitudes and rejections of hypocrisies, rather than to try and understand their goals and desires for progressive change.

To a major extent these rebelling young people, who for the most part are in the 15 to 25-year-old age bracket (and certainly not all "hippies"), include a vast number who have become disenchanted with authority—with our reaction to resist all change and to maintain the status quo. To them the rights of the individual to pursue his own goals are paramount. They look upon laws and rules as controls set up by "The Establishment" to infringe upon these rights. Love, sharing, acceptance, and involvement are basic to their philosophy. They believe that love and involvement rather than disinterest and exploitation should dominate human relations; that the right not to conform should be accepted; that there should be less government control; and that the objective of human endeavor is in helping *all* mankind to better conditions.

Perhaps our greatest "hang-up" over the whole movement

occurs in the area of drug experimentation. As concerned and, hopefully, rational adults we are concerned not only with the possible side effects and permanent damage that may result to the individual, but the effect of widespread drug abuse on our social, economic and even political institutions. We are concerned with the effect drug abuse may have on the community and state, on technical advances and quality as well as quantity production (which may result in improved living conditions for more and more people), on our personal safety and the general orderliness essential to a modern industrial society founded on economically and politically democratic principles.

In good conscience (but equally bad example) we have to challenge the reasoning of this vibrant and vocal minority that have raised an incantation that since alcohol is legal, why not drugs? They contend, and with justification at this time, that excessive use of alcohol and sleeping pills by the adult population is more detrimental to national health (while overlooking, perhaps, the reality that their generation now exceeds the over-thirty-years of age population and that they are merely adding to the detriment by using more drugs including vast quantities of alcohol and pills).

Some, without a knowledge of history and the facts, say that legalizing drugs would remove a rebel posture and actually decrease use. They feel that if we have a right to choose a life style, so have they. And so it goes. Our efforts to impress them with wisdom grounded in the hard school of experience are turned away with disbelief and distrust. A large segment of youth (activist and nonactivist alike) just will not believe anyone over thirty.

Before we rush to condemn the younger generation, perhaps we should have the patience to wait until they mature a little and make some sense out of the crazy world they will have inherited. It is salutary to remember that Samuel Johnson once said to Boswell who was criticizing a third party: "The Lord God does not propose to judge man until Judgment Day."

We also should beware of applying a two-dimensional measure of right and wrong to the activities of young people without recognizing the large middle area which could be embraced by a more tolerant attitude. We have, after all, not made this into the best of all possible worlds, and it is quite possible that some of the experiments now being tried by youth may give society a somewhat greater sense of group involvement than it has hitherto had.

Society has always had its jesters and dissenting factions, and no culture has ever been or ever should be judged by their activities alone. But in some periods of history, the wisest youth have been constrained by the dead hand of conformity to narrow views; where there has been such lack of experimentation, the culture has become stylized and sterile. We may hope that the experience of a wider experimentation of our youth under more permissive modern conditions will eventually lead the wisest among them to make more creative and innovative contributions to the society of the future. Besides, the world they are making is not really ours, it is theirs.

WHAT IS NORMAL?

James C. Bennett, ED.D.

For "OPENERS" perhaps accepted definitions are in order.

Clinical definition: "Normal: Conforming to, or not deviating from, the usual or the average or the norm (the usual performance); hence, neither abnormal nor subnormal; not suffering from mental disorder or mental deficiency."

Webster's New World Dictionary definition: "Normal, Conforming with or constituting an accepted standard, model, or pattern; especially corresponding to the median or average of a large group in type, appearance, achievement, function, development, etc.; natural; standard; regular.

"Normal implies conformity with the established norm or standards for its kind (normal intelligence)."

Thus, the question becomes "Are people who do not conform to, or who deviate from, the usual or the average or the standard, not normal?" Are they, in fact, abnormal if they do not conform to the accepted standard?

Are these definitions of normality too limiting? Are the standards to which we apply these definitions too restrictive? What about those who do not conform to the median or average of a large group in type, appearance, and achievement? Does this mean that such persons are abnormal?

What ramifications does this have for the culturally disadvantaged, for minority group members, for nonconformists, for highly creative people?

In April, 1966, at the 43rd annual meeting of the American Orthopsychiatric Association held in San Francisco, as reported by the *New York Times News Service,* several members questioned the accepted definition of normalcy and the concomitant categorizing of nonconforming as a pathological or abnormal condition. More than five hundred psychiatrists, psychologists, and social workers greeted those presentations with vigorous applause.

In discussing the student protest movement at Berkeley and active civil rights participants, a panel at the Orthopsychiatric Association meeting felt that while there were participants going along for the ride or for other vested interests, there was a core of participants who believed enough in a personal philosophy (that is neither illegal nor immoral and is based upon a sensitivity to man's suffering and a desire to attempt to improve conditions) that they were and are willing to back up their beliefs with dedicated action. They are willing to actually become involved in defending their ideals and beliefs. One member asked "Do apathy and conformity mean normality?" Another asked "What is normal and who are the normal ones?"

A quotation from the *New York Times News Service* covering the meeting stated, "In subsequent discussion from the floor, speaker after speaker acknowledged his professional debt to the youth movement which, it was said, has forced a reexamination of assumption about sickness and normality. " Many psychiatrists, psychologists and other behavioral scientists felt that very likely in the past the field of psychiatry and the mental health movement in general have been guilty of too narrowly defining normal behavior.

A Stanford student attending the conference drew a sharp distinction between beatniks and radicals. "Beatniks disengage themselves," he said. "They want to be individual dissenters. Radicals like ourselves are active. If you really believe in your values, it's important to convey them to other people."

In the June 28, 1966 issue of *LOOK* magazine featuring California as a national laboratory of social change, the Senior Editor, George B. Leonard, stated:

> Many of the older generation would like to call a halt to all the changes that seem to threaten them. But they will not stop the game. For the new modes of living do not pop up capriciously. They are the varied but inevitable responses to startling environmental changes. . . . The age of conformity has ended. . . . You with teenage boys may have faced up to some of the superficial signs of the new diversity: a hefty 17-year-old, for example, wear-

ing tight satin trousers, lace shirts and long, curly locks. How does he dare? How can he grow up to be a real man? Here is news from California, and from all around the globe: That boy of yours has no intention of growing up to be the kind of man you are. He is, in fact, not particularly impressed with your world.

Some schools struggle against the new diversity. At a time when they could well devote themselves to improving the quality of their teaching, many principals and teachers waste energy relentlessly, courageously stamping out long hair. Other educators, too busy with education to fret over styles, ignore coiffure and learn something that will be useful in the coming age: The sky won't fall in. . . .

In the future, the words "job" and "work" themselves, will be drastically redefined. A person's interests, status and worth will no longer be measured by his "line," but by how fruitfully he is involved in the whole drama of living. His "job" will mean less than his growth in fields broadly defined as "personal relations" and "education." . . .

Stop to think of the wonders that have enveloped our young people. They were children during the golden age of written and cinematic science fiction—a window to other worlds, other forms of life, other ways of consciousness. Then Sputnik went up, and fiction became fact. They are the children, too, of advertising, that enormous and still underrated channel of communication that so dazzlingly displays the diverse wares of our civilization and that, as much as any other force, is making the new age arrive. The young will not believe you when you tell them there is only one way of doing or feeling anything. They have lost that old, secure faith in the impossible. . . .

Expanding everyone's abilities will be a chief concern of our national life. It is quite safe to say that the *average* student of the year 2000 will be considered, in today's terms, a genius. Here is one of mankind's oldest and most irrespressible dreams: that the limits of what we can *do* and *be* lie beyond the boundaries of the imagination; that each human being uses only a tiny fraction of his abilities; that there *must* be some way for everyone to achieve what is truly his to achieve. The dream has survived history's failures, ironies and uneven triumphs, sustained more by intuition than by hard facts.

Now, however, the facts are beginning to come in. Science has at last turned its attention to the central questions of human capacity, has launched a search for a technology as well as a science of the human potential. LOOK interviews with 35 leading brain researchers, psychologists and educational innovators (more than half of them in California) reveal a firm consensus: People use less than 10% of their abilities. . . .

A spirit of hope is in the air. What comes of it depends not only on the wisdom of national leaders but on the acts of all who read these pages. Those who turn away still cannot escape the challenge. Those who have the courage of their humanism will rejoice.

While some of the statements by *LOOK* magazine Senior Editor Leonard, may be considered extreme by some individuals and groups, the fact does remain that a highly respected national organization such as the American Orthopsychiatric Association and a magazine of national repute appear to be challenging some of our concepts in regard to "normality" with newer concepts that eventually may lead to a broadened definition.

Perhaps the best we as educators, and especially as counselors and as pupil personnel workers, can do at this time is to realize that when we are attempting to draw a conclusion as to whether an individual is "normal" or "not normal" in a given area or situation, we must understand that we are referring to *only one area or situation* and that our conclusion can apply *only in that context*. We may not generalize from the one area as to the normality of the total person without examining all of the components that comprise the entity or the total picture. Quite possibly, science hasn't developed to the degree, at this time, where we are able to examine all components and draw such a conclusion. In making such a statement, it is understood that there may be exceptions such as certain types of psychoses where the condition may permeate the entire structure of the individual.

Another example of what appears to be a broadening of concepts as to what is considered normal is occurring in the test construction area; especially in regard to intelligence tests. During the past fifteen years, research has given us new insight into the nature of intelligence. This new knowledge has important implications for the content and essential character of intelligence tests. If these new discoveries are given the attention they merit, we have the promise of discovering intellectual potential that has been previously overlooked in our young people.

A major contribution of this research is the realization that our traditional intelligence tests sample only a relatively small portion of the factors that are involved in intellectual potential. These tests emphasize abstract thinking and reasoning ability, and place a premium on verbal comprehension and speed of response. They insist on the one "right" answer, and neglect completely the opportunity for original or creative responses. If we wish to recognize *all* intellectual potential, we must examine our measuring instruments, and revise them and modify them if necessary.

At the University of Southern California, research by J. P. Guilford and his associates has been especially impressive. A dramatic advance was his development of the brilliant three-dimensional theoretical model of the Structure of Intellect. This model hypothesizes 120 unique and distinct intellectual abilities. During the past several years, extensive research involving factor analysis has already verified the existence of approximately seventy of these separate abilities. It is quite possible that education in the future may be conceived as the stimulation of whatever of the more exotic factors of intellect an individual may present, on the theory that this is where the youth has the greatest potential of making an outstanding contribution. As we now stimulate such unusual athletic abilities as in the case of a Willie Mays or of a Joe Namath, we may someday stimulate the special intellectual factors of ability presented by some child now called "abnormal." After all, Socrates, Michelangelo, Wagner, Thoreau, Lincoln and Edison all had something "abnormal" about them.

Some may distort our views and say that to champion nonconformity is to condone immorality, atheism, un-Americanism, etc. We wish to go on record as opposing that which is clearly immoral, illegal, or unethical. But mankind in a world of change will make insufficient progress if we stereotype every kind of diversity as bad because it is "abnormal." Rather, educators, in general, and counselors and other pupil personnel workers, in particular, have a real responsibility not to blame "abnormal" behavior but to try to understand how it arises, what social and personal problems or issue it signifies, and what may be its outcomes. The abnormal behavior often signifies that the individual is out of touch with adult society. It can also mean that adult society is out of touch with the individual. As counselors and pupil personnel workers, it is our job to keep both of them in touch.

LEGAL POSITION OF SCHOOL PERSONNEL ON DRUGS AND NARCOTICS

Thomas A. Shannon

ALL OF US ARE WELL AWARE of the increasing illicit use of drugs and narcotics by our children. We are dismayed over reports from the probation department and the schools detailing not only the great numbers of kids involved in drugs or narcotics violations, but also giving evidence that there is *no* clear pattern of family background, neighborhood environment or economic status which would serve to assist the schools and other authorities to devise simple and effective programs of rehabilitation or prevention. In short, at this time there is a certain element of bewilderment and confusion about the underlying causes which impel some kids to flee into the world of Fantasmagoria via use of drugs and narcotics. In tandem with this bewilderment and confusion, there is a hesitancy about how to proceed at all levels of government, and among private agencies in the community, to develop programs which will deter the child who has never tried the stuff and rehabilitate the child who has.

Our State Legislature has *not* miraculously been immunized against this bewilderment, confusion, and hesitancy about youthful drug and narcotics usage. Assembly Concurrent Resolution No. 41 of the 1968 California Legislature candidly describes the quandry our legislators, who, for the most part, are practical and action-oriented men, are in on the subject of drugs, when it states:

> . . . Evidence presented to the Legislature indicates that there does not exist at the present time sufficient knowledge or experience which would allow the Legislature to determine with any degree of certainty what type of program (to treat and rehabilitate persons who use drugs and narcotics illicitly) could be most effectively developed and administered by the state. . .

92

Of course, this does not mean that the State Legislature has been sitting on its hands in the field of legislation controlling drugs and narcotics use. In fact, no less than a dozen laws concerning drugs and narcotics were passed by the 1968 State Legislature, ranging from clarifying criminal law sanctions against marijuana use to establishing a State Research Advisory Panel to coordinate research projects on marijuana. The language of Assembly Concurrent Resolution No. 41 *does* illustrate that the State Legislature is still shopping for a sound approach. And local public education has *not* escaped the attention of the Legislators.

During the 1967 State Legislative Session, Assemblyman Pete Wilson introduced a bill which ultimately was enacted into law as Chapter 1629. Section 1 of this law enjoined the State Department of Education to:

> undertake a study, in cooperation with the State Department of Public Health, on the subject of more effective education, including methods of instruction, relative to the physical and psychological hazards of narcotics and other harmful drugs and hallucinogenic substances, including, but not limited to, the question of the age at which instruction should begin, how often programs should be repeated, and whether programs should be taught by medical and law enforcement personnel, rather than by regular members of the faculty.

Under Mr. Wilson's bill, preliminary findings of the State Department of Education in its study must be reported to the Legislature March 15 of every year, until March 15, 1971, when the *final* report of the Department is due.

Against this backdrop, the question naturally arises: What has the Legislature done to control drug and narcotics usage among our children? Basically, State legislation on drugs and narcotics may be divided into three broad areas:

1. Those laws designed to stiffen and clarify the criminal statutes aimed at apprehending and punishing illicit drug and narcotics users, distributors, and manufacurers;

2. Those laws aimed at giving school authorities more discretion in dealing with public school pupils who wrong-

fully use, distribute, or manufacture drugs and narcotics; and,

3. Those laws attempting to gather information about the causes of drug and narcotics usage so that sound preventive and rehabilitative programs may be formulated.

For purposes of this discussion, we will concentrate on the latter two areas; that is, the legal bases for controlling pupils who illegally use drugs and narcotics and developing preventive programs within the organizational framework of the public schools. But, before we focus on the control of pupils illicitly using drugs and narcotics, it would be worthwhile to study for a moment the *kind* of pupil we are attempting to control.

In a recent study by Scott C. Gray, Director of the San Diego City Schools' Guidance Department and Dr. Richard Barbour, Assistant Superintendent, Student Services Division of San Diego City Schools, it was concluded that:

> Drug offenses are not, in the main, committed at school or by a hoodlum element having previous police records. The problem is not acute at present below senior high school. It cannot be related to an immigrant element. It cannot be related to intellectual deficiency or to low socio-economic level. The poor scholarship shown at the time of arrest seems attributable to the narcotics involvement rather than the narcotics involvement being caused by the poor scholarship.

This study suggests that the pupils whom the public schools are attempting to control in the area of drugs and narcotics can hardly be classed as the dregs of society forever condemned to hopeless lives because of the complete absence of potential to be successful in life. As we shall see, the State Legislature has given you broad discretion in controlling pupils who wrongfully use drugs or narcotics. This discretion must be used wisely and, in proper circumstances, with mature restraint, because your school disciplinary actions can have a profound lifetime impact on the pupils with whom you deal.

The authority of a California public school to discipline its pupils for wrongful activity with drugs and narcotics is specifically set forth in Section 10603 of the Education Code, which declares:

> The governing board of any school district may suspend or expel, and the superintendent of any school district when previously authorized by the governing board may suspend, a pupil whenever it is established to the satisfaction of the board or the superintendent, respectively, that the pupil has on school premises or elsewhere used, sold, or been in possession of narcotics or other hallucinogenic drugs or substances, or has inhaled or breathed the fumes of, or ingested, any poison classified as such by Schedule "D" in Section 4160 of the Business and Professions Code.

Let us now consider some practical questions concerning a pupil whose actions would seem to come under the provisions of this section. We will attempt to resolve the questions using the language of this section, and, where necessary, *other relevant* legal authority. The questions are:

1. *Must drug or narcotics offenses be committed while the pupil is under the supervision of the school?*

The answer is clearly "No." Section 10603 expressly authorizes suspension or expulsion from school of a pupil who has wrongfully "used, sold, or been in possession of drugs or narcotics while on school premises *or elsewhere*." In sum, the Legislature has concluded that if school authorities are of the view that continuance of an offending pupil in school would be inimical to the good order and discipline of the school, or adversely affects the education, even though the offense was committed away from the school, then the school authorities should have the power to suspend or expel the offending pupil. It is a matter of discretion with the school authorities. The test should be: Does the continued presence of an offending pupil negatively affect the discipline or education of the school? If the answer is "Yes," it is difficult to see how the pupil can be rehabilitated within the school, at least for the short run. It is also difficult to justify the contiuued presence in school of the offending pupil at the expense of the education of his classmates.

2. *What are the evidentiary standards which the schools may*

use in determining whether a pupil has wrongfully used, sold, or been in possession of prescribed narcotics or drugs?

Education Code Section 10603 authorizes expulsion or suspension "whenever it is established to the satisfaction of the (school) board or the superintendent" that a pupil has done the prohibited act relative to narcotics or drugs. This provision places any decision on the matter entirely within the discretion of school authorities. Therefore, an eye-witness account, an arrest for narcotics or drug violation, a report from a responsible person, *all* may be used as the basis of a suspension or expulsion, providing, of course, that the basis used was reasonable and the action taken was not tainted with malice.

3. *Does the law require a formal hearing before a pupil may be suspended or expelled for a drugs or narcotics violation?*

Statutory law may require a hearing in *expulsion* cases. Education Code Section 10608 provides for an appeal from a local school board's determination of expulsion to the County Board of Education. This statutory right of appeal has persuaded some attorneys that a local school board must offer a pupil the opportunity of a hearing in an *expulsion* case.

Parenthetically, the San Diego City Schools offers every pupil proposed for *expulsion* the opportunity of a formal hearing at which the pupil may be represented by legal counsel. The hearing is conducted by a hearing board of three experienced school administrators and an appeal may be taken to the Board of Education.

In *suspension* cases in *below*-college-level schools, however, *no* formal hearing seems to be required by law. Most school districts throughout the United States do *not* offer suspended pupils a hearing. As the U.S. Court of Appeals in New York said just last year in *Madera v. Board of Education of City of New York*:

> Law and order in the classroom should be the responsibility of our respective educational systems. The courts should not usurp this function and turn disciplinary problems involving suspension into criminal adversary proceedings—which they definitely are *not*.

Here in California, the State Supreme Court refused to hear an appeal on February 15, 1968, from a pupil in a case where the San Francisco Superior Court held that the arrest of a pupil on suspicion of throwing a fire-bomb in a school hallway was sufficient grounds for the accused pupil to be suspended from school without any kind of hearing.

4. How long may a suspension of a pupil for wrongfully using, selling or being in possession of drugs or narcotics be?

Education Code Section 10607.5 places a general total time limit of twenty days' suspension per school year for any pupil. This total time limit may be exceeded only in four situations: (a) when a pupil is transferred to a continuation or adjustment-type school, a suspension may be for the duration of the current semester; (b) when a pupil is transferred to another regular school for adjournment purposes, ten additional days of suspension are authorized; (c) when an expulsion of the pupil is being processed and the local school board has not yet rendered its decision in the matter; or (d) when an action against the pupil is pending in Juvenile Court and the court has not yet rendered its decision, a suspension may be for the period ending with the decision.

5. May the school records relating to the suspension from school of a pupil who has wrongfully used, sold, or been in possession of narcotics be expunged or sealed??

Section 781 of the California Welfare and Institutions Code provides for the expunging or sealing of records relating to juvenile law violators after a five-year period. When a sealing order of the Court is served on your school district, you are under a legal obligation to comply. You should gather up all records relating to the suspension and destroy them.

6. What is the relationship of the San Diego County Juvenile Court and the schools in the disposition of cases involving pupil drug and narcotics violators?

The maintenance of good order and discipline in a high school in which there are enrolled hundreds of impressionable, volatile teenagers is a complex and delicate job entrusted by California law only to specially educated, experienced, and licensed persons who are present on the high school campus all day all year long. The *judicial* processes, necessarily and properly including built-in time lags, third-party advocates, away-from-the-scene objectivity, relative disregard for the dynamics of immature group reaction, technical rules of pleading and evidence, and provisions for almost endless appeals, are hopelessly inappropriate for the task of controlling school discipline. California law recognizes this simple and clear-cut fact by vesting control of discipline matters of the public schools in boards of education, and *not* in the juvenile courts.

While the juvenile court disposition of a case involving a particular pupil does *not* control the discipline or placement of that pupil in school, both agencies are fully aware that they are dealing with the same juvenile. Therefore, close liaison characterized by mutual respect for each other's role in dealing with youth exists between the schools and the San Diego County Juvenile Court. However, notwithstanding the high esteem in which the Juvenile Court is held, under no circumstances should a school board abdicate its statutory responsibility of governing its schools and controlling the discipline of its pupils. Nobody understands or appreciates this fact better than the San Diego County Juvenile Court.

So far in our discussion, we have been concerned only with the negative aspects of pupil involvement with drugs or narcotics. That is, we have considered various legal questions which only arise *after* a pupil has been discovered illicitly using, selling, or being in possession of drugs or narcotics. The sanctions mainly involve suspension or expulsion from school or transfer of the offending pupil to a continuation school or a *different* comprehensive high school. We know that these actions clearly are *not* the entire solution to the problem of illegal narcotics and drug use by the youth of our schools.

Therefore, during the remaining time let us turn our attention to the *legal* bases for developing a sound educational program which will have as its purpose the discouragement of pupil usage of drugs and narcotics. In the words of *Drugs and the Caltech Student,* a booklet on drugs and narcotics published by the California Institute of Technology for the use of its students:

> The Institute . . . is an *educational* institution and believes that it can help students grow in wisdom, maturity, and responsibility more through educational means than through punitive or disciplinary ones.

The statutory basis for the development and introduction of an educational program in the public schools about drugs and narcotics is contained in Chapter 182, Statutes 1968. This law is officially known as the "George Miller Jr. Education Act of 1968" but is informally referred to as "SB-1." It has appropriately been described as the "Magna Carta" of local public education in that the State Legislature has indicated that it no longer intends to act as the master school board of California. Instead, the State Legislature has said, in Education Code Section 7502, which was revised by the "George Miller Jr. Education Act of 1968," that:

> The Legislature hereby recognizes that, because of the common needs and interests of the citizens of this state and the nation, there is a need to establish a common state curriculum for the public schools, but that, because of economic, geographic, physical, political and social diversity, there is a need for the development of educational programs at the local level, with the guidance of competent and experienced educators and citizens. Therefore, it is the intent of the Legislature to set broad minimum standards and guidelines for educational programs, and to encourage *local* districts to develop programs that will best fit the needs and interests of the pupils.

The "broad minimum standards and guidelines" for the educational program on drugs and narcotics are contained in the "George Miller Jr. Education Act of 1968" at Education Code Section 8503, 8504, and 8505, as follows:

> a. *Sec. 8503:* The adopted course of study shall provide instruction at the appropriate elementary and secondary grade levels and subject areas in . . . health, including the effects of . . . narcotics, (and) drugs . . . upon the human body.

b. *Sec. 8504*: Instruction upon the nature of . . . narcotics, (and) restricted dangerous drugs as defined in Section 11901 of the Health & Safety Code . . . and their effects upon the human system as determined by science shall be included in the curriculum of all elementary and secondary schools. The governing board of the district shall adopt regulations specifying the grade or grades and the course or courses in which such instruction with respect to . . . narcotics (and) restricted dangerous drugs as defined in Section 11901 of the Health & Safety Code . . . shall be included. All persons responsible for the preparation or enforcement of courses of study shall provide for instruction on the subjects of . . . narcotics, (and) restricted dangerous drugs as defined in Section 11901 of the Health & Safety Code.

c. *Sec. 8505*: Any course of study adopted pursuant to this division shall be designed to fit the needs of the pupils for which the course of study is prescribed.

Effectively, the "George Miller Jr. Education Act of 1968" has statutorily imposed upon local school districts and county departments of education the responsibility of formulating educational programs on drug and narcotics usage. While it is true that school districts have been required by State Statute for many years to provide instruction on drugs and narcotics, there has never been in force a legislative directive that school districts innovate and experiment with creative and imaginative educacational programs tailored to local needs.

In essence, the "George Miller Jr. Education Act of 1968" embodies a whole new way of thinking by the State Legislature. This new way of thinking by the lawmakers may be perhaps vividly summarized this way:

For years, school people have asked for more discretionary power in formulating educational programs for the public schools. They claimed they were humpbacked under the burden of state educational program-mandate piled upon state educational program-mandate. They said that the State prescribed such full and detailed educational course requirements that they had no opportunity to be less creative or imaginative in designing at the local level form-fitting educational programs for *local* needs. If only the State would back-off a bit, and give local educators room to innovate, the quality of local public education could not help but be enhanced.

Ladies and Gentlemen, the State *has* backed-off—through the "George Miller Jr. Education Act of 1968." The State has not abandoned the field, as we can see by Assemblyman Pete Wilson's Bill for research on narcotics and dangerous drugs by the State Departments of Education and Health, and Assembly Bill 195 of the 1968 Regular Session of the California Legislature which is now on the Governor's desk awaiting his signature. AB-195 appropriates $40,000 to the University of California

> for purposes of designing and implementing a research program related to the effects of marijuana use . . . in all pertinent research perspectives, including, but not limited to, pharmacology, physiology, and sociology.

But the State *has* backed-off in the sense that *no* longer is the old shibboleth of "The Education Code doesn't authorize it" valid in the case of educational program development. In fact, the whole future of local public education depends on how the "George Miller Jr. Education Act of 1968" is implemented at the local level. If the challenge of the Act is not adequately met at the local level with the formulation of effective educational programs, such failure will provide the State with persuasive reasons to centralize education in our State. And this centralization could take the form of abolishing local school districts and school boards as we know them today and replacing them with one statewide school district governed by a State Board and administered by a regionalized bureaucracy. In other words, the "George Miller Jr. Education Act of 1968" has given local public school districts all the "local control" they have been asking for over the course of many years; they are on probation and must exercise this newly found local control wisely and vigorously, or it will be taken back and lost to them forever.

There is *another* dimension to the problem. The Winton Act, passed in 1965 by the California Legislature, gives teacher organizations a "voice" in the formulation of educational policies in local public school districts. The teacher organizations, quite naturally, are anxious that their voices be heard. And school boards, the members of which are elected by vote of the people and whose responsibility is only to the people, have shown themselves ready to listen to whomever is capable of articulating sound educational program proposals and acting upon such proposals, regardless of how such action may seem to violate cherished notions of "going through proper channels."

Perhaps this is a new kind of healthy competition which will spur on *both* administrators and teachers to outdo the other in aborning creative and imaginative educational programs for our schools. Or, perhaps it signals the birth of an era of collegiality or participatory administration in the management of the public schools. Or, perhaps it signals the beginning of a good old-fashioned branigan between management and labor in the classic labor law sense. Only time will tell. Whatever it means, though, you can count on at least one fact: if the administration of a school district does not provide imaginative and vigorous leadership, the resultant vacuum will be filled, for better or for worse, by teacher organizations. And this is as true for drugs and narcotics education as it is for remedial reading.

In conclusion, the legal position of school personnel with respect to drugs and narcotics may be summed up in a few words:

> The discretionary authority given you by the State Legislature is extremely broad in pupil disciplinary actions—and you are empowered to expel or suspend pupils from school as you see fit, providing of course that you are acting reasonably and without malice. In a more positive vein, the State Legislature, in an historic move, has *formally* and unequivocally recognized your professional expertise in developing sound educational programs at the local level to meet the challenges of our new era—and one of these programs involves education about drugs and narcotics. You have all the legal authority to develop such programs that you could ever wish for. The Legislature is asking that you "do your thing." If you do *not* exercise that authority, or "do your thing," it will either pass over by default to teacher organizations or will be retaken from you by the State.

That is your legal position.

DRUG ABUSE—A SCHOOL DISASTER AND A PROBLEM FOR GUIDANCE*

Herbert O. Brayer

FOR THOSE OF US who read newspapers, magazines and watch television, there is little need to emphasize to guidance personnel or school counselors that school districts in every part of this nation, including Alaska, are face to face with a "Drug Abuse Epidemic." The alarming and unabating increase in teen and subteen use of dangerous substances, drugs, narcotics and hallucinogens has filtered down to the third grade in some instances, while drug knowledge and lingo is expressed unabashedly by youngsters in both the kindergarten and first grades. Unfortunately, we have evidence of where misguided adults have even sought to "expand" the minds of their own two- and three-year olds by deliberately turning them on with LSD and other hallucinogens. Many of you will recall the widely publicized account last year of a "learned" university professor who had not only given his children "acid" but had left some laying around so that while he was absent one day the youngsters turned themselves on. Let me assure you these are not unusual situations.

During the course of the past year we have had occasion to discuss this disastrous problem—for such it is to school authorities and teachers, as well as to parents and community agencies—with public and private school students on every grade level, with their parents, church leaders, juvenile authorities and law enforcement officials. We have attended scores of seminars, workshops, and taken part in at least a dozen panel discussions the result of which always has seemed to add up to

*This paper was presented as part of a panel session at the American Personnel and Guidance Association Annual Convention, April 2, 1969, at Las Vegas, Nevada.

the ultimate question, "What are the schools doing or going to do about this catastrophe?"[1]

There is no denying that schools are having a problem with drug abuse and drug abusers—both in school, and, because of specific laws, out-of-school abuse. In California, State laws specifically mandate teaching the evils of drug misuse, and the State Assembly has set up in the State Department of Education a special study with the specific charge of developing a state recommended educational program against drug abuse for the public schools. Despite the often heard comment by some still unconvinced educators that this is not a school problem, the plain truth is that it has been made one not just by law or directive but by disturbed and concerned parents and the upset community. It is much too late to either wait for the "thing" to "just dry up and blow away" or to deny that it is not "our problem."

Accepting it as "our" problem, however, fails to define "whose" problem in education it actually is. Of course, it is the problem of the members of Boards of Education, of Administrators—both district and those in individual schools—but the plain nitty-gritty of the matter is that these good ladies and gentlemen do not do the teaching or counseling with students. We do, and the purpose of this panel discussion today is to try and highlight for your consideration and active discussion the responsibility, or if you will, "our role" as guidance and counseling personnel in the handling of the drug abuse problem.

In doing so, and at our chairman, Dr. Demos' suggestion, I shall divide this presentation into two parts. First, a plan—already in use in some districts in California—for handling the student who has already been "busted" and for whom administrative action is pending. Secondly, I should like to present for

---

[1]The problem is not confined to the public schools. The writer has frequently this past year had occasion to discuss the drug abuse situation with officials of private schools including the parochial institutions. Parents cannot "escape" the drug problem by transferring their children to private schools any longer. Almost without exception these schools are having to face up to the same problem!

your consideration a generalized outline of an entirely different approach to drug users embodying a different philosophy and approach than the first. It is only fair to state that this second plan has not been, as yet, refined or adopted—or even really discussed by my own administration or Board—but it is one which I intend to present to them for consideration during April.

In the first instance let us make these assumptions based on rather widespread practice in various parts of the country, particularly in California. Assume that a secondary student has been "busted"—revealed by the police, school administration, or parents—as a drug abuser. The Board policy calls for a thorough investigation, a faculty-administration recommendation for action, and the final decision of the Board to (a) expell, (b) suspend, (c) transfer to a segregated "Continuation School." For the moment let us not become involved in the controversial questions relative to such a policy, but for the purposes of this discussion assume that this is the framework in which the counselor must operate. What could be the most effective role he/she plays in these very usual circumstances?

Our survey indicates that the usual procedure is initiated by the principal or vice principal. Based upon his information he generally suspends the student pending a hearing at which the parents are present and, in our district at least, they may bring an attorney with them. While clearly pointing out that the investigation and hearings are not judicial in character, every effort must be made to afford the student "due process" and recognition of his personal rights.

It is at this point that the student's counselor should become a "key" figure in affording not only "due process," but in seeing that the administration and the special hearing committee ("Faculty-Administration Placement Committee" generally made up of an administrator, counselor, teacher and, in one instance, the Assistant District Superintendent) receives a detailed but comprehensive "picture" of the student as an individual—a citizen in the school community.

A competent counselor would now fulfill the role and functions so well outlined by Dr. Harold D. Richardson in his recently published "operating manual" entitled *Developmental Counseling in Secondary Schools.* You will recall that Dr. Richardson specifies these as (a) the Individual Appraisal Function, (b) the Information Function, (c) the Counseling Function, (d) the Consulting Function, (e) the Follow up Function, and lastly, (f) the Evaluation and Research Function. In what follows I am taking some liberty in redefining these as they might relate specifically to the Counselor and drug abuse.

Ideally, as soon as the school administrator (principal or vice principal) is informed of the positive involvement of a student with dangerous substances, narcotics, or drugs, he would promptly notify that student's counselor (along with parents—and, if Board policy dictates, the authorities). It would then become the counselor's function to look into the source and degree of the charge. (a) What is the evidence? Was the student actually caught using, holding, pushing, in company with others using but not actually doing so himself? Is the source of the information reliable? Is the "evidence" positive? (We have seen instances in which the authorities were in error and it is possible for others to be mistaken![2]) (b) The counselor, following a preauthorized routine thoroughly clear to all concerned and always in writing, would then arrange for a prompt hearing (within 24 hours, if possible), by contacting the youth's parents and informing them of the precise time and place. A sincere attempt should be made to accommodate the time to the parent's situation. There is going to be enough "heat," and the counselor will do well to keep it "cool" from the very outset. Simultaneously a confirmatory registered or certified letter for-

---

[2]It is not the intent here that the counselor would become an investigator or detective in the police sense, but an "educational researcher"—one who wants the facts and an understanding of the background and all pertinent circumstances, not opinions, educated guesses or even strong suspicions. We recognize that the role of the counselor here is a difficult one—indeed we may in fact be discussing a new breed of counselors—but the intent is to differentiate between the function and the purpose from that which would be the case were this placed in the hands of the "decision makers"—the administrators. Ultimately, of course, the administrator would receive the results plus the rationale of the counselor. It is hoped that this would make the actual decision making more effective and valid.

mally stating reason, time, and place of the hearing should be mailed to the parent. ("Due process" again!) (c) Implementing his "informational" and "appraisal" functions the counselor would undertake an objective in-depth investigation of the student's academic and behavioral record. This he would do by his personal review of the student's "cum file," noting down pertinent facts shown in that record, interviewing teachers who have, and who have had, the student in class, referring to the health record, seeking information concerning extra-curricular activities in which the student may have been engaged, and identifying and problem areas—academic or behavioral—which might shed light on this particular student's risk-taking or aberrant behavior. Frequently information regarding specific peer group attachments (or the lack of it in instances of "loners") will have significance. The Counselor should interview the student and in his discussion seek information which can explain or shed light on his school, family or personal problems and drug involvement.

(d) Armed with such pertinent information as he has been able to assemble the counselor would now prepare a summary of the record and his investigations for presentation to the investigating committee. He may include his own impressions and possibly his own recommendations along with the documentation. It would not be unusual for him to turn up circumstances and situations previously not reported that will help the student. Circumstances have been found wherein the purported involvement was simply erroneous, unsubstantiated by "hard" facts, or beyond the accused student's control. In any case the appraisal, information, counseling and consulting functions would be used by the counselor objectively—to provide not just the bare truth, but understanding help for the, youngsters where justified.

There is a sincere difference of opinion (and rightly so) as to whether the student's counselor should be a voting member of the faculty-administrative committee and take an active role in the student's hearing before the committee. Some thoughtful counselors feel that to do either could compromise their future counseling with the student (who might now see him as a part of the prosecution process, or the "establishment.") Another objection might be that it could embarrass future counselor-parent relationships for the same reason. Indeed, there is merit in both of these objections but there exists also an equally concerned group of counselors who feel that since they had researched the case, they should have a voice (or a vote) in the discussions and recommendation of the committee. (It should be carefully noted that this is a "recommendation" and that the final decision-making is left where it belongs, in the hands of the administrators, the superintendent and the Board of Education.) Generally, the committee can recommend to the superintendent and the Board (a) returning the student to class because of circumstances or a lack of proof of direct drug involvement, (b) transfer to a continuation school, (c) suspension or (d) expulsion. Under the California Educational Code, the Board makes its decisions irrespective of legal actions that may still be pending or which have already been taken by the police or the courts.

Our concerned counselor, however, has not completed his role even though the student has been segregated, suspended or expelled. In most areas the student, after a short period or at the end of a semester or school year, can petition the Board to return to regular school. (In some instances—such as in our district—on the recommendation of the continuation school principal and teachers, or the superintendent, this time may be shortened or lengthened by specific board action.) In any event the counselor will again take an active role in meeting and counseling regularly with the "returnee" as well as counting this function while the student is in continuation school. During both of these periods the function of the counselor is of primary importance; indeed, the future of the student may actually depend upon how well the counselor fulfills his role.

May I now turn to the second phase of this presentation, a suggested plan for meeting the problem of the drug user through a decidedly different "educational" approach. It should be remembered that this is a purely schematic presentation designed to seek your assistance in finding a better approach to the school age drug abuser than those now in vogue. (To our knowledge the plan in the form now presented to you is not yet in use anywhere.)

A "CONTRACT" APPROACH TO TEENAGE DRUG ABUSE

The need for finding a "new" approach to the teen and subteenage drug user and abuser is greater today after three years of increasing youth involvement with dangerous substances, drugs and hallucinogens than at any time in history. While recognizing that the ultimate—if such there ever be—cure for the problem lies in a dynamic approach to drug misuse prevention through a combined operation involving parents, community, school and church and government, something much more effective than present methods must be found to help the great number of students already involved with drugs. This is an imperative; it cannot be further delayed without society being prepared to accept a drug-oriented generation with all that would entail for all concerned. The following "plan" is not a cure-all; it but suggests a start which, with initiative and foresight might be improved and altered until a much better plan has evolved. But it—or something akin to it—must be started now!

It is recommended to the Board of Education that, as an experimental alternative to our present segregation and penal approach, a broadened guidance program be adopted which will directly involve school counselors, administrators and effective volunteer teachers in a remedial as well as a preventative approach—not just to the "drug problem" but to its underlying causes. Recognizing that the schools can only do a small part of the two tasks of preventing drug abuse and providing effective therapy for those already involved, the plan envisions the active participation of parents as well as the direct involvement of the community.

Shorn of the details of operation in order that its outline can be briefly stated this, then, is our suggestion:[3] In lieu of segregating those students identified as involved directly or in-

---

[3] A detailed operations design will be supplied upon request.

directly with dangerous substances and drugs and popping them into continuation school as well as involving them with police, probation and juvenile authorities we are recommending that the Board consider a one-year test of the following:

1. When a student has been identified as a user and his parents shall be offered an alternative to present continuation school programs. This would be a *joint contract* under which the student and his/her parents would agree to a "Plan of Therapy" during which the student would receive individual evaluation initially with the determination as to his suitability for group therapy.

2. At the same time his parent(s) must agree to regular weekly attendance on the same day or evening as their son or daughter at a mixed group session composed of both parents and teenagers. For obvious reasons no student would be in the some group as his or her parents.

3. The duration of attendance of the parents and students "in therapy" would depend on several criteria (a) measured attitudinal changes determined by the use of a number of instruments now being tested or in preparation; (b) evaluation of the student's behavioral patterns over a period of at least one full academic semester; (c) clear evidence of a determination by parents to adopt an ongoing program of effective communication and genuine understanding designed particularly to the needs of their own offspring.

4. In this program the school counselor would play a very substantial role. We see him as directly involved in the individual as well as group counseling whether that program be set up as primarily within the school, or, as we would prefer, as a cooperative school-community venture purposely held outside or off the school premises.

5. While this program would take full advantage of all

agency and institutional experts as resource persons invited to participate in specific group discussions, primarily only competent guidance personnel would direct groups and do the actual counseling. These would include trained and experienced and well-screened school counselors, social workers, psychologists, sociologists, social anthropologists, minister, priest and rabbis with specific training and ability, and other social and behavioral scientists and teachers.

6. Each student would be assigned to a specific counselor whose initial task it would be to prepare a complete evaluation of the student and to lay out a suggested plan of individual and group "therapy." The plan would then be reviewed by all the participating counselors at a special meeting called to consider and approve that specific plan for that specific student. After its approval by the counselors the participating psychologist-consultant would review the plan, approve it or suggest alternatives and return it to the assigned counselor for implementation.

7. Now the counselor would meet with the student and his/her parents and complete the "contract." While retaining a signed copy, the counselor would file the original in the student's "cum" file, deliver a copy to parents and student, and send a copy to the office of the District Superintendent for informational use only.

8. If the contract is breached by failure to attend weekly sessions either by the student or the parent, or by continued involvement with dangerous drugs or mind-altering substances, or continued association with persons known to be involved with the "drug culture," the counselor will promptly convene a board of evaluation made up of the other counselors in the program, plus a school administrator. This board shall consider the failure to perform under the contract and recommend, in writing,

further or augmented therapy or that the Board suspend or expell the student or refer him/her to the appropriate juvenile or probation authorities as an "incorrigible."

9. Upon certification by the appropriate counselor—based on counseling group evaluation—that the student had shown definite attitudinal and behavioral improvement, and, that his/her parents had completed satisfactorily their portion of the contract, the Superintendent would terminate the contract and return the student to full standing in school.

10. If, as recommended, this program is set up by the school district and community jointly, the contract should include a flexible scale of fees to be paid by the parent during the course of "therapy." This will have the dual purpose of (a) helping to support the program and make it possible to reimburse counselors and participants on a "reasonable fee" basis, and (b) make the "bite" felt so that both student and parent will place more value on the "therapy." "It is a fact that most people value little that which they get for nothing. If they have to pay for it they will value it more, and since it has a monetary 'bite' to it they are more likely to take positive steps to see that the costly experience is not repeated." (If held as part of school activities the plan probably could not be charged for as far as the student is concerned, but there could be a fee for the adults.)

11. Coronado already has sufficient professional counselors and behavioral science specialists available to launch this program and the cost to the school district would be relatively small. (Details are available on costs if interest in the plan warrants.)

12. This plan has the salutary effect of combining the joint responsibility of parents, community, school and the

student in a positive approach to drug misuse with the possibility of a much more realistic therapeutic result than present methods.

It would be foolish, of course, not to recognize both the difficulties and limitations of the suggested program. It would also be remiss were we not to recognize in it the opportunity to get away from our present ineffectual program—ineffectual in attacking the drug problem. It is time to seek alternatives that have a potential for effectiveness by recognizing individual needs and differences. Perhaps this plan is not the answer, but it offers the opportunity to evolve from it more effective approaches designed specifically to help students rather than to just segregate and penalize them. It provides a way to keep the student in the central stream of education, not tossing him aside or relegating him to lesser educational opportunities.

It largely relieves the Board of Education and school administrators of hundreds of man hours of "due process" meetings, discussions, reviews and decisions which they now find not only burdensome, emotionally-charged, irritating, and unpleasant, but which also frequently leave them dissatisfied and dubious of the end result. It puts the problem of the immature student back where it belongs, in the hands of those who are trained and dedicated to educating him to solve his problems. It does this with a minimum of red tape, expense and stigma.[4]

COUNSELING WITH THE DRUG ABUSER

George D. Demos and John W. Shainline

FOR THE PAST SEVERAL YEARS we have attempted to counsel with a large number of young people who have become dependent on drugs of one kind or another. Our counseling contacts have been both within the college setting and in the framework of private consultation as well. The success we had to date is difficult to evaluate, but our failures are not, because with these particular young people (where we failed) our counseling and/or therapy was no match for the "glories" of dependency on drugs. With those young people, we have lost or are in the process of losing the battle to their sometimes fanatical missionary zeal for drugs. However, we believe that with continued research, study, and involvement, we will increase our chances for success with each drug abuser whom we counsel. Some of our colleagues in psychiatry and clinical psychology have said that traditional counseling or even out-patient psychotherapy cannot hope to compete with drugs as used by the chronic users, and that the best approach may be an extended period of institutionalization.

Perhaps the establishment of specialized hospitals for youthful drug abusers may be the only answer to treating the "hard core" confirmed multiple drug abusers. This, of course, will not eliminate the necessity for therapy, counseling and other helping modalities with the youthful occasional drug abuser who is not chronically dependent on drugs.

On the basis of the experiences we have had, and from our study of the approaches utilized by professional colleagues working with youthful drug abusers, we offer some suggestions in the hope they can be added to by others who have had some

---

[4]This brief outline is now being reviewed and evaluated by a group of experts and will be revised in accordance with their recommendations.

success in this, one of the most challenging problems of our time. It is suggested that before we attempt to counsel with the youthful drug abuser, we offer some questions to be asked of ourselves:

1. Do we have a knowledge of the drugs being abused and their effects? There is no quicker way to lose our youthful audience than to not have accurate information about drugs.

2. Do we have a knowledge of the language, music, etc., of the drug culture? Be aware of and understand what young people are talking about through their media.

3. Do we know the attitudes and values of drug abusers? Can we empathize with the youth who think their answers will be found in chemical substances?

4. Can we accept temporarily the client's abuse of drugs without early condemnation? Can we accept him as he is? This is particularly important early in the counseling relationship. To reject the client at the outset may hinder the possibility of his continuing. Once a relationship has been solidified, it may be appropriate for confrontation or more powerful leads to be utilized.

5. Will the fact that he is abusing drugs hinder us from establishing a trusting relationship? What are our attitudes about drugs? Do we have blind spots, prejudices, etc., about drugs?

6. Do we understand that we also have abused and continue to abuse drugs (of a different kind)? This is particularly true of alcohol and nicotine (both being drugs).

7. Can we be authentic in our relationships with youth—who put such a high premium on this quality? Hypocrisy and phoniness are integral parts of the credibility and/or generation gap that has evolved in recent years.

8. Can we strive to concentrate on the drug abuser's strengths and attempt to bring out his creative potential wherever present and wherever possible? We are usually so intent on changing his weaknesses or shortcomings we frequently forget his strengths. Let us never lose sight of the fact that this young person before me is in the "process of becoming" and on this long journey there are many way stations; let us not become fixated at one derailment.

9. Can I be open and truly honest with this individual before me—one who may have broken the law? Can I also admit to myself that I may have done the same under different circumstances (traffic, liquor, etc.)?

10. Will the fact that the client may be engaging in illegal drug abuse activities create a barrier of repugnancy which can deter our effectiveness in the counseling relationship? Let us try not to judge or to evaluate too early or too harshly. Let us try to understand!

11. Have we and do we continue to learn and understand the many complexities involved in what is referred to as alienation? This represents the single most salient factor relating to the social and psychopathology of drug abuse. More of the youth we have counseled fall within the category of alienated youth than in any other area. We must know and understand what it means to be alienated, and that a warm interpersonal relationship is the antidote.

12. Can we look beyond the symptoms (his behavior) and delve into the *why* of his actions to better understand the dynamics or motivating forces that are impinging upon him. Let us continue to look beneath the surface and search for causes of behavior—not to offer rationalizations, but to provide insights wherever possible. These are the therapeutic agents that really bring about change!

If we can, in our very difficult function and responsibility of self-evaluation, answer positively to a majority of these questions, then perhaps we are ready to counsel with the youthful drug abusers.

As with so many youthful clients, we visualized a great part of our role as counselors as centering around changing their self-concept. This so often involves helping the client over a "discontinuity" or transition from one aspect of role function to another, where hopefully the client's self-concept is changed from seeing himself in a nonperformance role to seeing himself in a self-assured competent performance role. (Gowan, 1967). It seems that so many of the youthful drug abusers see themselves on the sidelines and it is our task to help them see themselves as people who can and do perform. Some suggestions are offered as being pertinent for effecting the desirable change in self-concept.

1. Listen and give attention and regard to the client as he struggles, no matter how disguised his problems, to get to his problems—to get them out—to express them. Are we aware that simply listening to a client's problems helps him to talk about them and to better handle them due to his possible change of evaluation of himself?

2. The most troublesome and feared problem is that which can't be talked about. Drugs have considerable shock value and sometimes young people are reluctant to discuss their drug experiences with "squares." Once a problem is talked about, however, usually it is likely to lose some of its fear element for the client.

3. If we can get the client to reach into himself for the underlying reason or reasons for his dependency on drugs, we may then expect to have a real basis for a change in his self-concept. If his drug abuse is motivated by his fear of being unpopular, and all too often he does have a true picture of where he does or can

stand with his peers, his fear of relating or interacting with other people also cause him to search for easy solutions that give him a temporary respite from human interaction.

4. We need to help the client see that many other young people struggle with similar problems, but they labor to overcome these problems without resorting to drugs, and that drugs will be a hindrance to finding a solution to his problems. A number of clients on drugs often seem to save time by telling us that their problems are unique and are "bad"—"real bad," and not like anyone else's. If we can help him realize that others are like himself in their problems, this in itself will be a powerful force for a possible change in self-concept.[1]

5. We must be constantly conscious of discovering his strengths and endeavor to build on these strengths. With most of our youthful clients we *can* find an area where he is competent. In a school or college setting, it is sometimes possible to have his friends come to recognize and value his particular skills. Group experiences can be extremely valuable in helping the client appraise himself more realistically and frequently "point up" hidden talents.

Once again, basic encounters, sensitivity groups, marathons and simple group counseling experiences are strongly recommended in helping the drug abuser see himself. It can also help him "break through" the dreaded alienation so many drug abusers experience.

---

[1]One of our clients, after discussing point 4, offered the following: Individuality and personal uniqueness are of primary importance to youth in general today. Being his own person with his own talents and thoughts and problems is the essential concern of the modern day rebel youth. It is possible that quite a few of your clients would rather approach their problems in an entirely personal and isolated manner, i.e., in viewing their own situation as unique and their problems as their own, to be treated that way and not like anyone else's. (Even though, in fact, they may share like problems with other youths.)

6. Is the client really seeing himself in realistic perspective—"see-ing himself as others see him"? So often the youthful drug abuser appears to have a very warped view of how his peers really view him. When on the drug high, he loses this fear (fear of what others think), but it is inevitable that it returns once he comes down.

7. It appears almost universally with the drug abuser that he is not accepting himself as he is, even though his rationalization is that it is the fault of others. We must help him accept himself as he is, and if necessary, compensate for it.

8. It is important with the drug abuser to recognize the moment of contact when it is appropriate to instill confidence through encouragement and the right moment when necessary to engage in confrontation as to his weaknesses—his unacceptable behavior; his use of drugs. The choice of the right moment requires great care on the part of the counselor because failure here may mean a continuous dependency on the drugs and a turn-off from counseling.

9. Confrontation as a therapeutic tool with the drug abuser should be used sparingly in the counseling relationship, and only when the counselor is experienced and knowledgeable with regard to its possible or likely outcomes.

10. Confrontation is frequently interpreted by the drug abuser as a strong rejection and frequently causes either defensiveness or temporary compliance depending upon the status of the counselor, the dependency of the client, or the circumstances under which it is used.

11. Confrontation is likely to engender dependency in the drug abuser in view of its being an extremely strong lead, and the client is thus likely to look for other strong leads and direction on the part of the confronter.

12. Confrontation as a therapeutic modality, particularly in the hands of the novice, is more likely to be an expression of hostility rather than understanding, empathy or positive regard.

13. Confrontation is frequently justified by the counselor as being "open and congruent," but it may be an expression of rationalized aggression on the part of the confronter.

14. Confrontation is more likely to engender *less* insight on the part of the confrontee than more understanding leads—such as understanding remarks, interpretation, reflection, acceptance, etc.

In conclusion, what we are really attempting to do in our counseling relationship with the youthful drug abuser is to help him find a more constructive, less painful, and healthy way to go through the maturational process which can lead to positive and constructive change in self concept.

Finally, we must diligently try to communicate to youth that there are no simple answers to the perplexing problems facing us. If only a pill did exist that would answer all of our problems—but this thinking is fantasy. We solve our problems by facing them head-on, squarely and realistically, confronting one another with the real world, and not through a prism that distorts reality in the "eye of the beholder" (Demos *et al.* 1968).

Perhaps this is the lesson that young people must eventually find out for themselves; it is desirable to search for the truth, and there are no better ways than reality confrontation and hard work. The wishful thinking or magic formula panacea surrounding drugs may temporarily cause one to focus less on the real world—but the problems do not go away, and in most cases, they reappear in more complex forms.

The key words of the psychedelic cult: "turn on, tune in, and drop out," represent irresponsible and defeatist attitudes—a fatalism that, in our opinion, is escapism and, in very blunt terms, is stupid behavior.

A more vigorous, dynamic and viable approach would be

to *turn on* one's potential to cope with the problems facing us in our society; *tune in* to what we are doing and become more sensitive to the world around us; and *drop in* to the "real world" versus the fantasy world of drugs, and take a more active role in ameliorating its shortcomings.

REFERENCES

1. COHEN, SIDNEY: *The Drug Dilemma*, New York, McGraw Hill, 1969.
2. DEMOS, GEORGE D.: Drug abuse and the new generation. *Phi Delta Kappan.* Ohio, Otterbein Press, 1968.
3. DEMOS, GEORGE D. and SHAINLINE, JOHN W.: *Today's College Student in the Process of Becoming.* New York, Chronicle Guidance Publications, 1969.
4. DEMOS, GEORGE D., SHAINLINE, JOHN W., and THOMS, WAYNE: *Drug Abuse and You.* New York, Chronicle Guidance Publications, 1968.
5. GOLDBURGH, STEPHEN J.: An eclectic approach with hypnosis in the therapy of a drug addict. *Psychotherapy: Theory, Research and Practice.* Volume 5, #3, Fall, 1968.
6. GOWAN, JOHN C.: Effecting change in the self-concept of exceptional children. Feb. 1965, *Education,* Indianapolis, Bobbs-Merrill, Co., Inc., pp. 374-376.
7. NOWLIS, HELEN H.: *"Drugs on the College Campus."* Michigan. Drug Education Project of the National Association of Student Personnel Administrators, 1967.
8. ROGERS, CARL R.: *On Becoming a Person,* Boston, Mass., Houghton-Mifflin Co., 1961.

PARENT APPROACHES TO TEEN AND SUBTEEN DRUG ABUSE

Herbert O. Brayer and Allan Y. Cohen, Ph.D.

INTRODUCTION

George D. Demos, Ph.D.

T HE PROBLEMS OF DRUG abuse among our youth are legion. The authors of this pamphlet have enumerated some excellent approaches that can be of considerable help to parents in dealing with both prevention and treatment of the problems of drug abuse. Young people, in the final analysis, will have to make the ultimate decisions regarding drugs for themselves. However, we need not permit these most important value judgements to be made on a chance basis. There are some constructive approaches that can be utilized by parents which will provide the basis for decisions to be made wisely when they are confronted with the "magic" of dangerous drugs.

Unfortunately, there are no simple answers or no panacea to the apparently epidemic problems of drug abuse in our society. I commend the authors, however, in developing some very frank, clear and extremely helpful approaches, if practiced by parents, to ameliorate the problems of drug misuse.

PARENT APPROACHES TO TEEN AND SUBTEEN DRUG ABUSE

1. Have frank, open and frequent family discussions about drug use and abuse.

2. Adopt a sincere attitude of being a student yourself as far as drug matters are concerned:

   (a) be a student of drug use literature and educational materials;

(b) be a student of your children regarding the local drug scene; they'll know more about it than most so-called authorities;

(c) study challenging and zestful alternatives to drug abuse through discussion with your children; find alternatives that *they are interested in;* get reliable information not biased or propagandistic.

3. Don't "buy" propaganda and avoid moralizing—both turn students "off" and have little real effect.

4. Project confidence in your child or teenager's ability to make decisions. Teach them from facts how to make generalizations, to form attitudes, and from these to see values. Then teach them to use their knowledge and values in making decisions that only they can make for themselves.

5. *Be a parent,* not a buddy! *You* must establish the standards—the *values*—for your home. Your legal as well as moral responsibility lasts until your child is twenty-one or married! You and your spouse must set the "rules" of the game and these should be fair but firm. Insist on playing by these "rules" and don't let them fall into disuse. Your children must know what you expect of them—play, study, hours, clothing, deportment, manners, etc. So you will be a "square" to them . . . so what? That's better than being the parent of a "head" or dope user (or worse)!

(a) Know where your children are at all times and who they are with.

(b) Avoid *all* unchaperoned parties (beach, theater, mountains, slumber, etc.)

(c) Plan *family* affairs regularly and for your children (picnics, parties, outings, shows, athletic events, church, fishing, hunting, shopping, and theaters). Your grandmother used to say, "idle hands are the devil's workshop." You'd better believe it. But remember to obtain and maintain family identity on an "activity basis." Avoid "boredom" and "there's nothing to do on this island."

(d) Plan and demand "responsibility." Children can't mature as *responsible* persons unless given *responsibility*. Every child should have things for which he/she is responsible. The old but valued concept of "chores" or "duties" *is* character building. Authorities tell us these should start as early as possible—long before kindergarten. Remember, a child can't be responsible unless he knows responsibility (lawns, garden, room, dishes, yard, laundry or clothes, car cleaning or washing, etc.) These must be on a *daily basis,* not occasionally. Mother and Dad *must see* that these are really done.

(e) Be prepared for "I don't want to do it," or "I don't want to go with you Sunday," etc. As a parent *you are* the "boss." You must make being a parent work. (Again, it's better than being the mother of a drug-head, isn't it?) Resistance will go down proportionally as you insist on *your way* and as you explain your views and diversify your program. But it is too late to start this after your child has reached adolescence! Start as early in your boy or girl's life as possible—long before kindergarten.

6. Realize your importance as a model for your children! They want Dad as a "model" and Mother *is* their "model" despite other circumstances.

7. Give active support and offer real cooperation to community and school innovative drug abuse programs and projects.

8. Avoid arguing with your children about legalization or the legitimacy of drug laws; emphasize instead the per-

sonal effects (long and short term) of drugs on them personally and then on other human beings.

9. Separate the issue of drugs from the problems of the so-called "generation gap." Don't be trapped into relating these separate problems; it's like comparing apples and bananas.

10. Be prepared to work on your own problems of drug use and misuse; remember the proven facts concerning the drugs in tobacco, liquor, etc., that you may ingest regularly and which your children have learned are often worse for the human being than other drugs may prove to be. Don't excuse or hide *your* problem; be honest with your kids or expect them to use that ugly word "hypocrite."

11. Refrain from building your guilt complex over your children's drug abuse. Every youth problem isn't necessarily the result of parent failure.

12. Recognize and understand that drug use generally is sanctioned and even encouraged by American Society (alcohol, nicotine, caffeine, prescribed and nonprescribed mood drugs such as tranquilizers or "downers," amphetamines or "uppers," sleeping pills, diet pills, even aspirin, etc.)

13. When in doubt assume your child *is* experimenting with drugs. Don't panic, climb the wall, beat or throw your child out in the cold! Start communicating on a "*We* have a problem basis," and "how can *we* meet and solve it." Don't moralize! Your communication must be on a "man to man" basis, not on an outraged "criminal" one. Establish the rules of the game fairly and mutually. You can't run a prison successfully in your own home.

14. Be prepared to refer your teenager or child to proper agencies for emotional guidance and counselling—to

qualified people in the behavioral sciences such as psychologists, psychiatrists, physicians, social workers, school counsellors, or trusted teachers.

15. As a last resort—only *after* frankly explaining the reasons to the teenager—take him or her to the juvenile authorities and give them a complete and frank statement of your problem. Then follow their advice and don't try to "second guess" them.

16. During the next twelve months help meet the overall problems of your children and those of your neighbors' by taking an active role in forwarding the innovative educational programs planned by your local school district to meet the changing economic, political and social scene as well as needs of our young generation. We must more and more lay our stress on children finding and fulfilling their own potentials as against the grade orienting competition which is causing so many to either "cop out" or turn to drugs. Our schools must lay greater emphasis on teaching and materials relevant to the student's life and social problems as against the traditional transmission of facts for facts' sake. Your school board, administrators and dedicated teachers are working day and night to realize this program as quickly and effectively as resources, time and human energies permit!

But, they will fail miserably without your active concern and deliberate help on the "family front"!

SECTION THREE
CONCLUSION

CONCLUDING STATEMENT

James C. Bennett, ED.D.

In our symposium today we have seen the drug problem as one symptom of a seemingly disturbed society. This symptom manifests other symptoms of illness such as a high divorce rate, alcoholism, civil unrest, a general restlessness, and a lack of involvement. These problems depend for any degree of solution on positive and meaningful decision making on the part of all persons. We must make some decisions that will help our youth make better decisions, better than we have made in the past, if society is to continue and fluorish.

We need to ask, "What is the purpose of public education"? Historically this purpose has been to disseminate knowledge about the past. Today in order to produce responsible citizenship it is recognized that a curriculum focused historically must, in part, also be focused on the present. This means that our educational objectives have become broader in that they are concerned not only with factual data but also with the development of positive behavior in and among our youth. Today we are thinking of *involvement*—to involve the students, the school, the home, and the community all as one entity to help determine and to effect the whole spectrum of living.

Contemporary living can only be characterized as changing, changing at a bewildering rate. What should make up a contemporary curriculum? Should it not consist in assisting our students to ascertain objective and candid information (knowledge), in arranging opportunities for all manner of discussion, especially at the "gut level," in offering help in perceiving possible alternative decisions, and finally in acknowledging that these

EDITOR'S NOTE: Actually the concluding statement was made at the conclusion of the Symposium on Drug Abuse Among Youth In Riverside County. In this case it is being used as the concluding statement for this publication.

students will and must make their own decisions? It is impossible to write and rewrite textbooks and change teaching techniques rapidly enough. Our effectiveness lies in helping students gather information, discuss and assess, and finally allowing them to make judgments. These are tools they need and that must be emphasized. To provide this will require curriculum change. Only if constructive and needed change is built on the foundational tools just named can change be effective. We cannot anticipate the occurrences of the future, but we can try to prepare our youth (the adults and parents of tomorrow) with ways to act on these occurrences. Many areas of the current curriculum offer opportunities for fact finding, decision, and decision making, but not much of this deals with contemporary problems about which to fact-find, to discuss, or to decide. We need a continuous curriculum entitled, "Education for Contemporary Living," with coordinated programs from kindergarten through grade twelve. This coordinated curriculum must be involved with drugs, alcohol, tobacco, sex education, family life education, and especially with civic responsibility. What we are proposing may be a controversial solution to some people, but we must realize that the schools are in a primary position to assist students in taking their places in a complex society. No longer can we allow minorities of dissenters to keep us from this important business. Indeed, such a curriculum should be extended into higher education and into adult education.

The schools cannot initiate and sustain such a program alone. The school is the focus but it is not the backbone of the attack. The community and its agencies must not let the schools stand alone in times of crisis, but they must work with the schools and support mutual goals. Many of our community resources are ready to help. They need *assistance* and *coordination*. Community group concern begets individual volunteers.

Within the school system, direction and leadership are needed from school board members. This requires courage to be in the forefront of changing community attitudes. Superintendents, other administrators, and teachers can plan and participate, but they need the leadership and cooperation of the school board.

We must learn to listen to our youth. We will not turn our world upside down at the urgings of a few malcontents, but we will learn to cooperate with the majority of youth who can tell us valuable things in regard to their feelings about our culture. This must be a mutual quest, not a manipulation of one group by another. It makes a difference if we listen, understand, and trust.

This symposium is but a first step to deal with the problem of drug abuse. We have shown through our attendance that we are concerned, but programs can only come to fruition through continued dynamic leadership. School board members and the community are in a position to provide this leadership. The schools and other agencies must cooperate to work out the details. Only with such an effort can we hope to help young people move away from specious solutions (such as drugs represent) to the courageous solution of facing reality and making appropriate decisions. There is no alternative to this battle. We must win. Let us resolve that our continued concern will result in opening lines of communication that will help our youth prepare themselves to face the urgent problems that lie ahead.

AUTHOR INDEX

133

SUBJECT INDEX

A

Abcesses, 30
Addicted, 65
Addiction, 7, 12, 27, 29, 32, 33, 35, 38, 46
Addicts, 22, 27, 28, 30, 31, 34, 64
Administrator, 55, 71, 99, 105, 109
Adults, 46, 84
Alcohol, 20, 29, 34, 35, 36, 77, 84
Alcoholism, 32, 35, 129
Amphetamines, 7, 29, 35
Arrest, 18, 23, 56
  see also Juvenile Arrests
Aspirin, 29

B

Barbiturates, 29, 35
Bendzedrex, 29
Benzedrine, 29
Benign (ref. to marijuana) 14, 19, 20
Blood poisoning, 30
Bromides, 29
Bromo-Seltzer, 29

C

California Delinquency Prevention Commission, 12
California Rehabilitation Center, 28, 30, 32, 33
Campus, 24, 37, 47, 69
  see also College, School
Casa Blanca House, 47
Chloralhydrate, 29
Chronic, 15, 19, 39, 113
Church, 47, 48, 49, 108
  see also Clergymen
Classroom, 11, 51
  see also Education
Clergymen (inc. Minister, Priest), 38, 46, 48, 49, 63, 103
Cocaine, 29
Codeine, 28

College, 14, 68, 76
  see also Campus
Continuation School, 108, 109
Conviction, 13, 16, 17, 22
Cops, 51
  see also Law enforcement, Peace officer, Police
Counselor, 38, 44, 50, 51, 55, 56, 58, 62, 63, 66, 67, 81, 103, 104, 105, 106
Court, 12, 13, 16, 20, 51, 108
  see also Juvenile Court
Credibility Gap, 14, 22
Criminal, 15, 16

D

DARE, 79, 80
DAWN, 80
Defendant, 15
Delinquency, 15
Demerol, 28, 29, 46
Desert Sands Unified School District, 54
Deterrent, 14
  see also Prevention
Dexedrine, 29
DMT, 14, 29
Drug Abuse, v, 12, 20, 27, 28, 33, 34, 35, 36, 37, 43, 44, 48, 52, 53, 54, 77, 79, 84, 102, 109, 114, 119, 120, 131
Drug Abuse (a publication), 36
Drug addiction, (defined), 27
Drug use, 17, 34, 37

E

Education
  as institution, 43, 44, 45, 87, 93, 127
  see also School, College
  as means of solution, 7, 35, 54, 57, 77, 102, 130
  see also Prevention

135